THE DOUBLE CROSS

THE
DOUBLE CROSS

Ordination, Abortion,
and Catholic Feminism

❋ ❋ ❋

Denise Lardner Carmody

CROSSROAD · NEW YORK

BU
676
. C36
1986

1986
The Crossroad Publishing Company
370 Lexington Avenue, New York, N.Y. 10017

Copyright © 1986 by Denise Lardner Carmody
All rights reserved. No part of this book may be reproduced,
stored in a retrieval system, or transmitted, in any form
or by any means, electronic, mechanical, photocopying,
recording or otherwise, without the written permission of
The Crossroad Publishing Company.
Printed in the United States of America

Library of Congress Cataloging in Publication Data

Carmody, Denise Lardner, 1935–
The double cross.
1. Ordination of women—Catholic Church.
2. Abortion—Religious aspects—Catholic Church.
3. Women in the Catholic Church.   4. Catholic Church—
Doctrines.   I. Title.
BV676.C36   1986   282'.088042   85–29942
ISBN 0-8245-0736-3

For My Four Brothers:
John, Tom, Jim, and Rich Lardner

CONTENTS

PREFACE

I address this book, as I have my previous books on Christian faith and feminist allegiance, to centrists, people willing and able to think in terms of both-and rather than either-or. Moreover, I again address the median eighty percent or so of those interested in both Christianity and feminism—all but the very far left and the very far right. What is peculiar about this book, however, is that I work more directly from my own Christian tradition, that of Roman Catholicism, addressing two issues that disturb many Roman Catholic feminists. I assume that the issues of women's ordination and abortion disturb many people outside the Catholic Church as well, but in this work I have on my mind the peculiar problems that will occur to Roman Catholics. I do not assume that much more than a majority of my readers will agree with the stands I take. I do assume that these two issues involve the most crucial decisions Catholic feminists must face if they are to fashion a viable spirituality.

My thanks to Frank Oveis, of Crossroad Publishing Company, for sponsoring this book editorially and helping me focus it; to my husband, John Carmody, for editing and strong turns of phrase; and to the following feminists who have been a supportive circle: Joann Wolski Conn and Walter Conn, Helene Lutz and Bill Shea, Judith Plaskow, Rosemary Reuther, Elizabeth Clark, Mary Harren, and Bob and Sydney Brown.

·1·

INTRODUCTION

· CATHOLICISM ·

Among the major Christian groups—Eastern Orthodox, Roman Catholic, Mainline Protestant, and Fundamentalist—Roman Catholicism stands out governmentally for its reliance on papal authority. Spiritually, it stands out for its holism. "Catholicism" means "according to the whole" (*kata holos*), and we still use the word *catholic*, with a small c, to denote something that is universal in its outreach, broad or comprehensive in its concerns. So a person of "catholic" taste has many interests and accepts many styles. By implication, a feminism that is catholic ought to range widely but seek balance and comprehensiveness.

We shall reflect more on "feminism" in the next section. The main point I want to secure here, dealing with Catholicism, is the beauty I have found in what I take to be the better or truer instincts of Catholic Christianity. I am what used to be called a "cradle Catholic," born into one of the many ethnic ghettoes of pre–World War II Baltimore. My group was mainly Irish-Catholic, and my elementary and secondary education was in parochial schools. So intense an immersion in a subculture assures that one will know its spots and wrinkles quite exactly. It is only later, when one has lived in different subcultures and gained perspective, that the better possibilities of one's own group start to become clear.

The better possibilities of Catholicism radiate from its sacramentality. Along with Eastern Orthodoxy, Roman Catholicism has taken to heart the Johannine theology: "No one has ever seen God; the only Son, who is in the bosom of the Father, he has made him

1

known" (John 1:18). This stands over against the Pauline stress on justification by faith which has shaped so much of Protestantism. The two theologies are not incompatible, of course, but they do lead to two different religious styles. At its best, Catholicism is iconic, convinced that the divine Word and Spirit can vivify matter and make it the means of human beings' divinization. So the water of baptism, the bread and wine of the eucharist, the oil of anointing, and the flesh that spouses embrace can all mediate the warm light, the clear love that we instinctively feel is the best index of the divine nature. The candles that flicker on the altar, the incense that arises, the chant or polyphony, the gorgeous vestments and the rest have a radical justification in the Word's having taken flesh and dwelt among us, full of grace and truth.

Amusingly enough, one who grows up in this sensate religious tradition can come upon the bareness of a New England Congregational church or the silence of a Quaker meeting and feel a blessed relief. Also, one can leave the ghetto considerably scarred, for Catholicism frequently misses the mark and so does not achieve the incarnational balance postulated at its founding. In modern times this has been especially true regarding sex, with consequences for Catholic feminism that we shall have to consider in full detail. So I am not saying that Catholicism is the only way, or the best way, or a way with no serious deficiencies. As actually experienced, Catholicism can be as unauthentic or crippling as any other religious tradition. Equally, however, and as idealized, Catholicism can be as mind-stretching, adventurous, and beautiful as any other religious tradition. It has mystics who know silence as well as Quakers do. It has prophets and troubadours of poverty who understand to the marrow why New England Congregationalists wanted bareness. The Word of God that has riveted Protestantism to the Scriptures is inseparable from the sacramental words that Catholics feed upon. The Word that took flesh so situates any Johannine Christians in the world that nothing human is foreign to them.

My first instinct in starting on this theological venture, therefore, is quite positive. I have appreciations to vent, debts to pay, and I acknowledge them gladly. If there are dozens of things that I would redo in my early education, there are hundreds of good moments to recall. If I wish that my parents and teachers had been wiser and freer, I must in simple honesty confess that their faith was at least as strong as mine. My mother had only a grammar school education, yet she raised five children admirably. She lost my father when I was seven. She lost the second oldest of my four older brothers when he was eighteen (cannon fodder for General Patton). So in her early forties she was the widowed mother of four children, and she balanced her household accounts by making little piles of money in different drawers. She did not exist in the world of credit, having never borrowed her way into being. She died before she reached sixty, another victim of cancer. Yet you would have thought no princess had ever had a better life than she. Her faith had made her deeply eucharistic: a person whose first word to both the Father of lights and the Mother of God was gratitude.

Anthropologists could speak of my mother's Catholicism as "the little tradition" or even as "peasant faith." Liberation theologians today might classify it as "popular religion." It was alive with saints, novenas, and votive candles. It spoke to God and his Mother daily, treating them as intimates. The psychologist could say that my mother used her early morning masses or the times she slipped into a darkened church for a visit as therapy, as a way to let her troubles slip away into something bigger, a way to console herself with images from the way of the cross or intimations of a heaven where her losses would be restored to her. She would not disagree, but she would point out that her therapy (God's therapy, she would call it) was much cheaper and more highly recommended.

I have learned a great deal from the great tradition of Catholicism. The official dogmatic theology, as systematized by St. Thomas or St. Bonaventure, or as brought up to date by Karl Rahner or Bernard Lonergan, has given my mind precious light. Similarly, my heart has profited greatly from the writings of Teresa of Avila, John of the Cross, and the anonymous author of *The Cloud of Unknowing*. Yet throughout I have always been gratified to find a glimpse of peasant wisdom anchoring these marvelous higher developments. So it has pleased me to imagine Rahner visiting his hundred-year-old mother and going back to work on the next volume of his *Schriften* with advice perhaps to "eat your cabbage" or "get your collar cleaned."

I was delighted to see photographs of Bernard Lonergan as a boy. He had a full head of hair and a reputation for bullying his younger brothers. The people I have found wisest have not lived gilded lives, have not had their way smoothed by every advantage. They have learned wisdom by suffering. They have been forced to accredit the cross. So Lonergan's thesis that the intelligibility of redemption is a "law of the cross" through which God overturns the calculus of evil rings true in my center. The passover of Christ celebrated in each mass sets the beauty and grace of religion in the center of sacrificial love. We all die and we all suffer. None of us has ever seen God. All of us need a God who is holy, mighty, and immortal. All of us need the only begotten Son of God's bosom to make our sin and grace manifest.

These are some of the Catholic embellishments I hope to contribute in the reflections that follow. They are traditional confections or spices, but no less savory in our time. Fifteen or twenty years ago it was fashionable to speak of "man come of age," a secular city surging ahead. We know at least a little better than that nowadays. "Man" has hardly come of age when more than half the species are not equally represented by that generic term. The secular city is hardly the polis of progress when it has more crime than grace, more misery than mysticism. Without an incarnate divinity, a truly eschatological prophet, the bloom fades from our rose. We are then, of all recent generations (two thousand years' worth), the most to be pitied. Without catholic wisdom and outreach, we are far from liberated.

· FEMINISM ·

The first of my allegiances relevant to this book inclines me to hope. Catholic Christian faith is not an optimistic purveyor of "onward and upward," but it is deeply committed to the proposition that where sin abounded grace abounded the more. It does not accept the notion that human beings are depraved or radically untrustworthy. It reads the sign of Jonah, the risen Christ, as reason to bless all creation and to follow God in calling it good.

My second relevant allegiance is feminism, and I can say things about it that are quite similar to what I have been saying about Catholicism. Of course, I have only come to a reflective feminism in recent years. When I was growing up I accepted the fact that there were different school yards for girls and boys, that girls could not serve on the altar or be ordained priests, and all the other aspects of women's second-class status in Catholicism as simply the way things were. So, too, with the aspects of subjugation or inequality that formed me in the culture at large. I was more a realist than a prophet, better at learning the rules of the game than at scattering the marbles and forcing the rules to be rewritten. And I still suffer from having grown up in a pre-feminist time. There were losses in educational opportunity, religious opportunity, psychological confidence, access to economic and institutional power, and much more that I shall never recoup. I think it is as healthy to face these realities as I think it is unhealthy to beat them to death.

Most people, through the hundreds of thousands of years of human history, have been seriously disadvantaged. Most people have been undereducated and overstressed. Few people have not needed liberation or redemption. All people have had to contend with the evil of their fellows and the pains of their mortality. Have women suffered more than men? Have mothers had more pangs than fathers? Probably so, but who is to say? Men and women are so deeply entwined, so utterly coordinated with one another, that historically a push on one side of the sexual scale has meant a reaction on the other side. The *Tao Te Ching*, after millennia of human experience in Asia, stated very clearly that happiness, justice, efficacy and the rest are all very paradoxical. If the outside of the house gets all the attention, the empty space inside the house constitutes most of the usefulness. If the men bluster and parade in front, the women live longer and shape the race more deeply. The path goes its way, the wood follows its grain, and we are wise in the measure we learn from their example. Chuang Tzu knew that death returns all of us to the great clod of the earth, so Chuang Tzu refused to lament his wife's passing. Like Socrates, he couldn't be sure that the dying don't go to a far better destination.

In any adequate perspective, therefore, feminism has to keep its championing of women's equality well connected to history and mortality. The sexes have shaped one another since Eden, for better and for worse. In the latter millennia the outer shell of our story has had men as the leaders and oppressors and women as the followers and oppressed. I find this pattern both real and vicious in my American society of the mid-1980s, so I think that justice and faith require that we now try to redress the imbalance, giving women's side special attention and appreciation. (This is also true for blacks and other people not being dealt a fair hand.) This sort of effort to redress, attend, and appreciate is what I mean by "feminism." Were there no injustices, feminism would have little reason to be. Of course one could still rightly celebrate women's achievements, provide for women's bonding, and support women's special slant on wisdom, but there would be no need to do this as a prophetic cause or to plunge it into the pool of miseries that complete what is lacking to the whole Christ. Since there are these injustices despite considerable gains, feminism continues to be a moral imperative. In my opinion, not to be championing women's drive to become accounted fully equal to men in humanity is to be derelict in one's faith and morality. With war making, racism, and economic oppression, sexism shows us the face of Satan in our time.

The foundation of feminism, therefore, is our human thirst for justice. We are made to experience, understand, judge, decide, and love. If we experience suffering, understand it to stem from inequities, and judge that many of these inequities are culpable, we must move on and decide to try to change the presently unacceptable situation. Probably the best way to do this will be to come to show the victims of injustice a preferential love. In loving them—showing special tenderness toward their bruises, spending special measures on their restoration to full health—we will be loving the neighbor whom we can see. According to the canons of I John, this will keep us from being accounted liars when we claim to love the God whom we cannot see: "If any one says, 'I love God,' and hates his brother, he is a liar; for he who does not love his brother whom he has seen, cannot love God whom he has never seen" (I John 4: 20–21).

In my theological anthropology, the God we cannot see is present in our thirst for justice. The ideal reality that we project when we revolt against disorder, injustice, dishonesty, and all the other manifestations of human twistedness is what Jesus named "The Kingdom of God." We love the Kingdom of God whenever we choose light rather than the darkness, or choose the oppressed rather than the oppressor. We love the Kingdom of God when we move in the flow of feminism rather than sexism, when we support racial equality rather than racial discrimination. Each day movements such as feminism and anti-racism set before us two ways, one of death and one of life. Not to choose feminism, understood as the movement to redress the injustices women suffer because of their sex, is to choose death. Sexism, like racism and the inclination to make war, is radical irreligion. It is closure to the mystery of God that lures the human conscience, unwillingness to love and face the law of the cross.

To be sure, many secular feminists would be uncomfortable hearing that their movement, as a conscientious choice for light and life, is radically religious. To their mind "religion" is largely superstition. In its institutional forms, religion is even a major part of the problem, a major prop of the rotten cultural edifice that feminists have to tear down. So the distinction between authentic and inauthentic religion, Christianity, and feminism comes to center stage. People will use these terms differently or make different judgments about what is or is not authentic, but I do not accept the notion that this de facto disagreement makes all evaluations relative. The drive to experience, understand, judge, decide, and love is universal. It expresses an integral spirit—mind, heart, soul, and strength—that is either moving forward into the light and love of the mysterious God or is sidetracked, turned in on itself, suffering the perversion of Bergson's "closed soul." Eric Voegelin has described the basic movements of the integral human spirit that are crucial for mental health, and these make it plain that authenticity and inauthenticity are both solid realities and unavoidable terms.[1]

The crux of the feminism that I want to support, like the crux of my Catholicism and religion, is the rationality and love it is serving and developing. I don't care a great deal what feminists call themselves. They may be Christians or Marxists, secularists or believers, gay or straight, wealthy or poor, political or mystical. I care whether they are attentive, intelligent, reasonable, decisive, and loving. I want their actions to square with their words, their overall personality to ring true. If they are not honest or dependable, they are a menace. If they are filled with hatred they cannot cure. I prefer the profound agnostic to the trivial believer, the kindly mystic to the brutal politico. The one thing necessary is that they reject the injustices and oppressions women suffer and commit themselves to overcoming them with honesty and love.

· TWO CROSSES ·

Take a sacramental religion focused on Christ, add an honest commitment to equalizing women's possibilities, and you have most of what I mean by Catholic feminism. Move these commitments into the parade of current history, however, and you run smack into confusions and sufferings you could never have foreseen. Nothing in my essential sketch of Catholic feminism prepares one for the controversies now swirling in the Roman Catholic Church about the status of women. Similarly, nothing in it prepares one for the bitter battles about abortion that divide communities across the land. Both of these painful situations engage feminists and Catholics in special measure. So in my mind's eye they have merged to become a double cross, a twofold measure of trial and salvific opportunity.

The principal connotation of my title for this book is therefore soteriological. I see the questions of women's ordination (which can stand as the keenest edge of the question of women's status in Catholic Christianity) and abortion as two of the major trials that current history is forcing upon all who would confess an allegiance to both Christ and women's equality. For faith, these trials are of course a mixed blessing. They are painful, and so naturally bad. Only a sick religion would bless them unequivocally. But by the law of the cross they can become redemptive. By suffering through them in love—doing our best to change the evils we can and to accept the evils we can't change as part of God's inscrutable plan—we can remove much of their poison and show that God need never be defeated. The glory of the Johannine Christ, we frequently need to recall, is inseparable from his being raised up on the cross.

There is a second connotation to "double cross," of course, and I am not going to pretend that I don't also want to convey it. I think that Catholic feminists and others caught in the painful swirls of the controversies over women's ordination and abortion have frequently been betrayed. And, to be even more exact, I see the major betrayals as coming from two different directions and intersecting in a way especially painful for Catholic feminists. By the canons of authenticity that I have sketched, I find most of the opposition to women's ordination in the Roman Catholic church unacceptable. It is the ultimate resistance of a power that I think must now be called culpably blind to its significant role in women's oppression.

There will be space later to add qualifications to such harsh judgments, but right here I want to be unmistakably plain. Not to make the church a place in which there is neither male nor female, in the restrictive sense of the classical Pauline text (Galatians 3:28), is to default on the justice and love essential to Christian faith. It is to "hate" the sisters one can see and so strongly suggest that much of one's professed love of the God one cannot see is hypocritical. Where women ought to find in the church a championing of their fight for equality and justice, they often find ridicule and neglect, if not redoubled oppression. This is a double cross, a terrible failure to act as Christian principles proclaim that Christians should.

From the direction of secular feminism comes another serious burden for Catholic feminists. It is perhaps even more complicated and in need of further examination, but it too should be laid out in unqualified terms. Women certainly should find in feminism of any stripe a support for their proper autonomy or self-determination. They should find in any group possessed of common sense a great respect for their primary role in bringing forth new life and for the concomitant cluster of feelings and judgments that the symbiotic relationship of expectant mother and fetal child produces. They should not find an advocacy of abortion as a perverted rite of passage into feminist maturity. They should not find an indifference to fetal life that makes abortion an acceptable contraceptive. When abortion becomes simply another medical "procedure," all of civilized humanity suffers, but women most of all. For procedural abortion reduces women to the status of brood mares. What they carry is not more than animal life, and they are nothing but a means to a biological end. So however understandable may be the doctrinaire championing of abortion one often finds in feminist circles, by the standards of authenticity I hold it is deplorable. With friends like doctrinaire abortionists, women have more than a bellyful of enemies.

I would exaggerate neither the pains these crosses can create nor the willfulness of the groups—Catholic officialdom and secular feminists—who play major roles in their arising. Suffering is all around. Neither women's unjust treatment in the Christian church nor the pains created through abortions have a monopoly. I would agree with those seeking a seamless ethical garment that we have to see the connections among the nuclear arms race, the destruction of the ecosphere, the sufferings of the world's hopelessly poor, and all the other assaults upon the sanctity of life. On my own agenda abortion does not occupy the top line and the ordination of women would not be first if I were granted three wishes. But when I examine current culture in the crossing hairlines of Catholic faith and feminist allegiance, I find these two problems or scandals highly illuminating. Mulled over, studied through, taken to simplifying contemplation and sobering praxis, they have revealed a depth of disorder and a stubbornness of sin that make me call my previous views of the world naive. This has not brought me to the brink of voiding the blank checks I used to think we should write to God. It has not caused me to reject my faith that grace is more powerful than sin or that human nature is not depraved to the core. But it has shown me that liberation and redemption are not terms or realities we should toss around easily. It has reminded me of Bonhoeffer's distinction between cheap grace and grace that is won at cost.

The Bible, of course, has long told us not to put our faith in princes. The prudential or sapiential heritage of Israel and the church would have us trust only in the goodness and creativity of God. The two crosses certainly only find their proper frame when we set them in the context of the divine mystery. Without referring them to the mystery of the Beginning and the Beyond, we keep them on the level of a political football tossed back and forth by dialecticians. If we add the paschal form of the Christian mystery, they become even better focused, for we find that Christ too felt pain from quarters from which he ought to have received support. He came unto his own, but his own received him not. And he even had to question with the Psalmist why God seemed to have forsaken him.

This is the ultimate question that I see Catholics and feminists raising, although they are often not aware of where their turmoil has led them. If the church does not manifest the love of Christ, to what institution should one go? And even when one rightly refuses to define the church in merely institutional terms, the coldness or carelessness of one's fellow Christians can bring the same despairing inquiry. Similarly, if one goes to the sisterhood and finds lots of welcome and interest, but then is declared anathema because one's reverence for life casts huge brackets around abortion, of what use is the vaunted feminist support? And if one has had both experiences, as many Catholic feminists have, the question can become more cosmic: Is there any purpose under heaven for this so doubly crossed time? What is the Master of the Universe, the Lord of the Dance of Life, doing to redeem the so many "troubles" (to use an Irishism) of these times? The main reason my loss of naivete has not led me to stop writing blank checks to the divine mystery is that I find no sure answers to these all too legitimate questions. Like the absurdity of the arms race, or the sinful pollution of nature, or the spectacle of hundreds of millions of poor people lacking necessities while hundreds of thousands of affluent people chase after luxuries, they take one to an abyss that only the silence of God might comprehend.

· THIS BOOK ·

This book takes much of its character from the silence of God. I intend it to be an extended meditation or reflection, rather than an empirical or even analytical investigation. I want to mull over the significance of women's ordination and abortion, treating them holistically rather than separately, forcing them to thrust out tendrils of connection to other issues and values rather than letting them swell up to occupy the whole screen. Specialists in either of the two issues can supply far better than I exact details of law or refined ethical arguments. My sense, however, is that often such studies miss the mark that the feminist of lively Catholic faith finds central. The central issue finally is not a matter of laws or even a matter of rights. The central issue finally is a matter of the order or disorder that only right relation to the sovereign divine mystery can give. This mystery often seems silent, both in the sense of being beyond what words and ideas can touch and in the sense of perhaps not existing or caring, but this simply brings us back to a religious bottom line. That the most penetrating descriptions of the implications of the divine mystery come from people who have been willing to brave dark nights and clouds of unknowing simply says that nothing so fraught with difficulties as women's ordination or abortion can escape the twin demands for radical contemplation and radical politics.

I conceive of this book, then, as both generalist and religious. I also conceive of it as tolerant, tentative, willing to proffer the positions on which I now act but not willing to cast them in cement. The explosion of knowledge and self-awareness that has occurred in the past fifty years makes all of us amateurs. None of us can be masterfully competent when a problem has legal, historical, psychological, sociological, religious, and medical overtones. So we all have both to accept a tentativeness or imprecision in our judgments (without letting this paralyze us into inaction) and to find a way to undercut many details that are of only secondary importance, so that we can home in on the central issues. The tentativeness appropriate for this essay seems to me quite analogous to the "epistemological tolerance" that Heinrich Fries and Karl Rahner have proposed in the context of Christian ecumenism.[2] The undercutting of specific details that in the final analysis are of only secondary importance is reminiscent of Rahner's call for "short formulas" of Christian faith that might summarize the whole in a nutshell.[3] And the overall result? One can hope that it will aid people who realize that openness, connection to others, ongoing dialogue, further clarification of essentials, and resolute action all have to come together and cohere.

The traditional counsel that has guided many generations of Christians caught in the throes of disagreement comes to mind at this point. Where things truly necessary for the existence of the community are in question, one must insist on unity. Where things not yet clear or of dubious ultimate significance are in question, one should grant liberty or freedom of opinion. And in all things, grave or relatively unimportant, one should both insist upon and grant love. To be sure, the historical record shows that dissidents have found it difficult, indeed, to agree on what is essential and what accidental. They have seldom had tidy zones in which to practice now unity and then liberty. Even worse, they have regularly refused to make charity the universal ideal and requirement. But the dictum itself has great merit. It should force us to concentrate on essentials, letting our modern appreciation of historical relativism pry our fingers away from past dogmatism. It should remind us of Paul's clarion call in Galatians 5:1: "For freedom Christ has set us free," helping us put the burden of proof on those who would curtail Christians' or indeed any people's freedom. And it should teach us again, to our shame, that the only final criterion is the love, both rational and warm, that we show or don't show those with whom we are interacting. Epistemologically, this love is the force that keeps tolerance from being careless. As well, it is the edge or initiative that gets us inside concrete situations, with their often many tangles, to find the better instinct or motive that even the actors themselves may have overlooked.

In Part I, dealing with women's ordination, the traditional dictum should seem completely apt. The context is the Christian church, although of course current secular history intrudes, and if one cannot assume that the dictum is a faithful and authoritative translation then the game is lost before it has begun. To make the position grist for my meditative mill, I plan to take up four principal subtopics: Christian ministry, women's work, women's leadership, and women's priesthood. By thinking about them with what I hope is both faith and feminist commitment, I expect to wander my way (the terrain is hardly laid out in neat midwestern squares) to the conclusion that the difficulty women are having trying to achieve, through ordination, full ecclesiastical equality in Catholic Christianity is probably the key sign of that contemporary institution's sinfulness. Along the way, however, we should see interesting sights: scenarios of what a Word properly preached and a sacrament properly administered would look like; reminders of how central women's labors are to the most crucial tasks of procreation, education, and healing; provocative reflections on the styles of leadership that women tend to develop, which strike me as almost eerily appropriate for a time steeped in schizoid militarism; and a tableau of what women priests could be, what they now actually are, and what they imply for the whole ministerial dimension of the church.

Part II, dealing with abortion, will not take us completely outside the ecclesiastical circle, but it will more explicitly focus on secular feminism. First, I shall sketch what I consider aspects of the Christian world view that bear most directly on abortion. Then, I shall sketch what I consider the aspects of feminism theory that have the most direct bearing. Third, I shall weave back to Christian theology, asking for a prudential theology that deals with the realities that women now in fact experience in abortion. Last, I shall consider the political positions that the foregoing Christian and feminist reflections seem to suggest, emphasizing the complications introduced by a pluralistic culture whose primary value has been individual liberties.

The conclusion, which I conceive of as a mirror image of this introduction, will no doubt reveal the personal agenda that I have been pursuing throughout the entire meditation. I want to bring the two crosses, the two sets of baggage, to bear on the question of a Catholic feminist "spirituality," meaning by this term "reflective and passionate faith." The topics that have come to mind, as I anticipate this conclusion, are the radicalism proper to Catholic faith today, the new importance we should accord Lady Wisdom (as Rosemary Haughton has named the directive spirit we most need[4]), the authenticity that could be the meeting ground for Christians and feminists, and the surrender to the mystery that is proper to people trying to come of age. By this conclusion, I hope, the meditation will have stimulated readers to think about their own share in the realities being mulled. If so, it will have contributed something useful to the work of forming consciences—the work most crucial in a time when the ideological or doctrinaire formation of minds obviously is insufficient—and I shall be fully gratified.

* Part I *
ORDINATION

ORDINATION

In Catholic Christianity "orders" is a sacrament. The people chosen by the community to lead them, or selected by leaders already in place, are "ordained" to their tasks in a rite that stresses the laying on of hands and an anointing with holy oil. Both gestures are associated with invoking the Holy Spirit, who is to be the future leader and servant's best source of inspiration. Both gestures express the community's sense that the Spirit that has empowered it through past ages must come in tangible form to all new ministerial leaders, and that those ordained should be sealed or signed with the chrism of joy, the balm for sadness.

Nowadays the theology of orders in Catholic circles usually takes a somewhat Protestant turn, quickly emphasizing that all authority in the church of Christ is ministerial or for the sake of service. So Jesus is remembered to have said that he did not come to be ministered unto but to be the servant of all (Mark 10:45). So the rite of Maundy Thursday, in which the officiant washes the feet of others in attendance (ideally, of the poor), symbolizes the attitude most praiseworthy in church leaders. If all Christians are to be servants of God and their neighbors, the Christians who hold office in the church and most dramatically exercise authority are to be the servants of the servants of God. Popes, cardinals, or bishops, they should stand out for spending themselves that the community might not just survive but flourish.

The gains that an ecumenical sensitivity have brought to the Catholic theology of orders narrow somewhat, however, when one comes to the strand often referred to as "early Catholicism." This is the trend, clearest in the Pastoral Epistles (1 and 2 Timothy, Titus), to think of church leaders as principally conservators. For the Pauline school represented by the Pastorals, the presbyter or bishop in charge of the local community is first of all the guardian of traditional faith and morality. Several generations' worth of experience apparently had shown the necessity for tightening both doctrinal and ethical discipline, so the leader of the local community is painted in rather somber tones. One can see at least the seeds of the later hierarchical structure of the church Catholic, and faith is well on the way to being conceived as a "deposit" handed down from earlier ages. In this conception, the first task is fidelity to the tradition (the handing on). Innovation or spurring people to greater liberty is not high on the agenda of the Pastorals.

From biblical times through the history of Christian ministry[1] to our present ecumenical times, the content of "orders" therefore has been mixed or complicated. Church leaders were to be both servants and conservators. They were indebted to both the present community and the past tradition. Some of the imagery surrounding their office suggested that they should consider themselves the least important members of the community. Other images shouted that they were kingly personages, rightly clad in crowns and rich robes. As a result, people contemplating Christian ordination today may feel quite free to rethink the whole matter. Obviously they should take past notions of Christian ministry into account, but equally obviously those past notions have never come together into a chorus singing as with one voice. The more closely one considers the historical evolution of the Christian ministry, in fact, the clearer it becomes that the community usually affirmed its right to adapt ministerial structures to the pastoral needs of the given time. Clearly this was not a right completely open-ended or without constraints from scripture and past tradition. Equally clearly, however, there were sufficient changes from the formative generations of the apostles and evangelists to warrant the principle that the community has sovereign rights over its own ministry. If given ministerial forms are not serving the community well, the community certainly has, under the Spirit, the right and duty to modify those forms.

In terms of our discussion to date, this suggests that the particular forms that Christian orders or ministry has assumed down to the present era are not part of the invariant essence of faith or community life. One could argue that some form of leadership is of the Christian essence, but whether that form ought to be presbyterial or episcopal, more determined by the local community or more determined by previous officeholders, can hardly be considered essential. If, in Rahnerian terms, the three cardinal mysteries of Christianity are the trinity, grace, and the incarnation, with scripture, the church, and the sacraments best considered as (secondary) expressions of this cardinal triad, then certainly the particular forms through which people are ordained, or the particular structures through which they minister, can hardly be considered chiseled in stone for all time.

There is a hierarchy of truths in the Catholic scheme of things, and if one employs it the sex and marital status of the Christian minister are surely not primary matters. These questions have their significance, but it is far less than the significance of the inner being of the Christian God, or the free grace of the Christian God, or the astounding claim that the Christian God stands revealed once and for all in Jesus of Nazareth raised to be the Christ. Moreover, the significance of secondary matters is more often than not limited to their instrumental value. Their job is to mediate, proclaim, and render effective the great primary truths. So the church ought to take the forms, liturgical and governmental, that best enable it to be the city raised up on a hill, to be the community that sacramentalizes the humanity that the light and love of God would develop in all human beings. So the officers of the church ought to be chosen mainly for their wisdom and ministerial competence. Their sex or marital status, like their age or race, ought to be incidental and quite secondary considerations.

This is the rationale I shall bring to the chapters in Part I. The counterposition, which usually argues that ordaining women would conflict with longstanding Catholic tradition, seems to me untenable. (The arguments for requiring a celibate Catholic priesthood are even less persuasive, since the church's first leaders were mostly married men and the law of celibacy has always had numerous exceptions, especially in Eastern Orthodoxy.) Not only have recent feminist scriptural scholars opened wide the possibility that women led early Christian communities,[2] but recent appreciations of human historicity call into question the wisdom of letting a patriarchal past determine a present sensitive to feminist goals. In other words, even if there were no historical precedents for the ordination of women (and there are precedents, abundantly so in the Protestant churches), the current situation of the church—conceived of as the whole community of Christ's followers, and therefore as having a female majority—fully legitimizes the theological opinion that the part of wisdom nowadays is humbly to attend to the Spirit that a great many women say is active in their midst.

With this perspective in mind, I shall consider Christian ministry, women's work, women's leadership, and women's priesthood as lenses through which we may estimate the status of a Catholic feminism and try to discern how it ought to move. I shall not spend much time defending my assumptions that women may be as competent or spiritually gifted as men and that the pastoral needs of the community of Christ take precedence over canon laws or variable church customs. People who don't share these assumptions are not likely to follow me through to my concluding Catholic feminist spirituality, so all I can do is ask them to keep their adversarial reading friendly, as Christ certainly would enjoin.

·2·

CHRISTIAN MINISTRY

· SERVICE ·

If you asked a representative sample of people who they felt best exemplified the Christian faith in recent years, many names would probably be mentioned. Without doubt, however, they would frequently name Pope John XXIII, Martin Luther King, Jr., and Mother Teresa of Calcutta. For my present purposes, these three famous and justly praised exemplars of Christian faith make the case for the primacy of service better than could lengthy textual or theological studies. The "sense of the faithful," as theologians sometimes refer to the instinct that the Holy Spirit spreads through the community of Christians, has by vague yet powerful agreement found that each of these world-famous figures represents something at the marrow of Christian commitment and ministry.

Pope John XXIII, the supposedly interim pontiff who forever changed Catholic Christianity by calling the Second Vatican Council, was by no means adventurous or innovative in his theology or his piety. The new mark he brought to the Vatican rather lay in his personal warmth and openness. Whereas Pope Pius XII, for all his austerity and learning, never mastered the art of seeming to be the servant of the servants of God, and Pope Paul VI, for all his evident dedication to the well-being of both the church and the underprivileged, never showed the world the joy of discipleship, Pope John XXIII, fat and kindly, convincingly communicated that his office meant little in terms of personal glory. He was completely directed to expressing the love of God for all people, especially those who had felt themselves alienated from traditional Catholic Christianity.

Thus Protestants came to think of Pope John XXIII as one of their own most significant shepherds. Eastern Orthodox realized that the Vatican was finally serious about repairing the long scandal of East-West rupture. Jews rejoiced that the head of a church that had seemed to consider them Christ-killers would remove the most odious anti-Semitism of the Christian liturgy and speak to them as brothers. Even Marxists and atheists, who had for generations automatically assumed that the Catholic Christian faith was their antagonist, found themselves drawn to the humanity of Pope John, and therefore much more willing to consider Catholic invitations to dialogue. The liberalizing decrees of Vatican II which upgraded the Catholic opinion of Protestant churches also recognized the right of all people to religious freedom and accorded the convictions of non-Christian religious people sincere respect. These decrees received the support of Pope Paul VI as well as John XXIII, but the impetus to *aggiornamento* that got the whole process of opening the Catholic Church to the modern world going came completely from John. His worldwide popularity finally was due to the impression he created that in his pontificate authority was not there to preserve the institution he headed but was to serve all people's flourishing.

Martin Luther King, Jr., created a very similar impression. By the sheer rightness of his cause, his willingness to suffer for his people (first blacks, and then all oppressed peoples), his eloquent evocation of the biblical prophets, and finally his sacrificial death, Martin Luther King, Jr., convinced all people of good will that whatever office or status he held completely served the cause he had come to consider God's work for him. Like the early Christian leaders who have left traces in the biblical record, he enjoyed a charismatic or Spirit-given authority. It was not through a bureaucracy that he created change but through a nearly direct expression of a vision and a nonviolent strategy that came to him in prayer and deep reflection. As with Pope John XXIII, though, the key to his success was the ministerial stance he projected. The gifts he had and the work he did followed closely on the model of the Master who had laid down his life for his friends.

Mother Teresa of Calcutta, my third example of a ministerial worker who has achieved an enormous success, followed Martin Luther King, Jr., in winning the Nobel Peace Prize. Like him, she has been taken to heart by the worldwide community both for herself and for the attitude she symbolizes. In Mother Teresa's case the persuasiveness comes from the very wretchedness of the people for whom she has given her life. By ministering to the hopelessly abandoned and dying people of Calcutta, a city that redefines the meaning of human poverty, she has prodded the conscience of the world to reconsider its priorities and reacquire a reverence for all human life, no matter how bereft or derelict. Mother Teresa has asked virtually nothing for herself. She seems completely uninterested in personal power or glory. Her authority comes from the sanctity of her person and her work, and like the moral leadership of Martin Luther King, Jr., it is a nearly direct expression of the Holy Spirit who in times past raised up saints like Francis of Assisi, another great champion of the poor.

My point in mentioning these three recent exemplars of Christian faith has not been to dip into hagiography or throw my mite into the outpouring of praise. My point has been to dramatize the servanthood that so often is the crux of an effective Christian ministry. If people perceive that representatives of the Christian community genuinely seek to be helpful and are genuinely on the side of the poor and oppressed, people are almost forced to offer respect and openness. In contrast to the ministerial forces who ask for money while promising, with pearly smiles, physical healing or financial prosperity, my Christian exemplars cast their lot against the status quo and worked for radical changes that would make it clear that the Father of Christ is a God who cares for all people, especially the weak and downtrodden.

Edward Schillebeeckx has stressed the indissoluble ties between the Father of Jesus and the welfare of human beings:

> Like God, Jesus preferred to identify himself with the outcast and the rejected, the "unholy," so that he himself ultimately became the Rejected, the Outcast. This identification is indeed radical. So there is continuity between Jesus' life and his death. Precisely for that reason, Jesus' saving significance comes to a climax in his death. The theologoumena used in the New Testament and indeed later to describe this reality of salvation to certain people within their own culture should not be confused with the specific reality of salvation itself. The redefinition

which Jesus gave of both God and man, in and through his proclamation and way of life, takes on its supreme and ultimate
significance in his crucifixion: God is present in human life
where to human vision he seems to be absent. On the cross God
shared in the brokenness of our world. This means that God
determines in absolute freedom, from eternity, who and how
he will be, namely, a God of human beings. In his own being
he is a God for us! It is very difficult to find a distinction between God in himself and God for us in the New Testament.[1]

If the Master spoke of a God who is for us human beings, and if
the Master's fullest revelation of God's identification with us human
beings came on the cross, then surely authority in the community of
those professing to be the disciples of the Master wanders afield
when it ceases to conceive of itself as primarily a service, a ministry,
a *diakonia*. Leadership in the community of Christ ought mainly to
be formed by the paradoxical pattern of Jesus' own authority. In
contrast to the great powers of his time—or to the great worldly
powers of any time—he did not seek to lord it over others but to
place himself at their disposal, indeed to give his life to ransom the
many held captive by the oppressive power of worldly rulers and
Satan (the personification of anti-godly spirituality). So while competence in Christian ministry may include both an intellectual
mastery of the message of Christ and the wisdom that Jesus could
call serpentine, it finally refers to the persuasive powers of Jesus'
death and resurrection. The most credible mediators of the power
of Jesus' love will be those who most convincingly imitate his ministerial selflessness. Can anyone seriously argue that Mother Teresa
or dozens of other women wouldn't qualify for the priesthood of
this description?

· PREACHING ·

The substance of Christian ministry may be the credible service of
its ministers, but ministry has so evolved historically that preaching,
celebrating, and healing are tasks that co-define it. Apart from the
connection with the tasks that Christian ministry has assumed, one
finds it hard to define what Christian ministry means. The preaching that comes to mind in this context is not, of course, a pejorative

preachiness. The preaching that comes to mind is the heralding or proclamation of the good news of Jesus Christ.

This gospel or good news of Jesus Christ is itself several-sided. There is Jesus' own preaching, which mainly focused on the Kingdom of God. There is the early Christian proclamation that Jesus himself, as Lord and Savior, is the substance of the good news. And there is the historical aftermath of this early Christian proclamation, which scholars sometimes summarize by speaking of a tension between "already" and "not yet." Thus the word that Christian preachers are to proclaim in season and out is neither simple nor monotonous. For every season, it is a stimulus to search out God's effective will to be for us human beings, to offer healing and fulfillment.

Nowadays one of the most persuasive interpretations of the good news that the church should always be preaching stresses that the gospel should be an agent of liberation. Unless people find that the scripture being read out in church is a help in their struggle to free themselves from the forces oppressing them, then scripture has in effect become a dead letter. Unless people find that the sermons being preached in the church are a help in their struggle to clarify where they stand and where they ought to be moving, then those sermons are in effect a waste of breath. The people who live below the poverty line don't need pious talk about the dangers of mammon. They know mammon as the force that strews ghettoes and malnourished children in its wake the way a hurricane strews shattered houses. The people who inhabit the margin of the economic and cultural systems because their color or their sex is wrong need a gospel that speaks effectively of a conversion or a new creation, of a God who will wipe every tear from their eyes.

So, effective Christian preaching has a double focus. It surveys the example of Jesus and insists that salvation is already possible. Here and now, in this our own too familiar place, the love and life of which the Johannine literature speaks is active to reconcile enemies and make life good. Then and there, in the realm that the New Testament conjures up by speaking of resurrection, the sending of the Holy Spirit, and a deathless zone called heaven, the first fruits of Christ's victory will have become the completely pervasive redefinition of human possibilities. The Word to preach is balance, poise, both-and. The Word to preach is the Word made flesh, the hinge between heavenly immortality above and earthly limitation below.

What then does feminist theology, which is rooted in a perception of the liberation peculiarly needed by women, suggest about Christian preaching? First, that unless it summons the Spirit who drove the prophets out to seek justice, it lies unconnected to the great Christian dynamo. Luke's portrayal of Jesus' first preaching in his hometown synagogue of Nazareth puts this connection unforgettably: "And he came to Nazareth, where he had been brought up; and he went to the synagogue, as his custom was, on the sabbath day. And he stood up to read: and there was given to him the book of the prophet Isaiah. He opened the book and found the place where it was written, 'The Spirit of the Lord is upon me, because he has anointed me to preach good news to the poor. He has sent me to proclaim release to the captives and recovering of sight to the blind, to set at liberty those who are oppressed, to proclaim the acceptable year of the Lord'" (Luke 4: 16–19; Isaiah 61: 1–2, 58:6).

The gospel to be preached must be good news to the poor and release to the captive. It must restore vision to those who can no longer see, give hope to those who find the present age impossible. I will not say that women are a majority of the people in these categories, because the descriptions admit of spiritual dimensions in which women more often than not display remarkable resources. But I will say that progress from a fifty-nine-cent female dollar to a sixty-two-cent female dollar is not the accomplishment of women's economic liberation. I will say that a church unwilling to admit women as members fully equal to men is nearly as blind as a regime based on apartheid. As long as the economic indicators continue to predict that women and children will be the bulk of those living below the poverty line, honest preachers of the gospel don't need to do much research to declaim about mammon, sin, and injustice. As long as women are not represented in secular congresses or religious synods at levels equal to men's, the "not yet" of the Kingdom certainly outweighs the "already."

The principal reason why these topics are not prominent in the sermons preached in Catholic Christian churches is that few of the preachers suffer the injustices involved. The principal reason why we don't have the social gospel we should is that most of the people whom Jesus beatified live across the tracks from the priests and bishops. You can't preach what you don't know. It is hard to appreciate the liberating power of the gospel for women if the church doesn't consider women as equally fit for religious authority as men.

So the preaching of any ministerial group depends on much more than its learning or eloquence. At the center of effective preaching is the sort of penetration of the good news that only suffering servants or those highly conscious of having been liberated are likely to attain. The Christian church could solve the problem of ineffective preaching by simply stirring up the Spirit given to all church members at baptism. As the basic communities that dot the Latin American landscape suggest,[2] whenever people are forced to grapple with the connections between scripture and their own concrete circumstances they become preachers to one another. A dialogical process ensues, such that members of a little group build on one another's interpretations of the given scriptural passage and usually round out a balanced reading. This may not be "preaching" in the sense of handing exegesis down from an elevated pulpit, but it can certainly get the community as a whole to take the Word of God more deeply to heart.

When we deal with the priesthood women now are exercising in many Protestant churches I shall consider the preaching and other ministrations that already take place in feminist modes. Here let me illustrate women's proclamatory contributions by citing two of the women from Ernesto Cardenal's Solentiname community in Nicaragua who help round a discussion of John 8:1–11 (the episode of the woman taken in adultery) into a fully liberating analysis:

Teresita: "I believe all the men who were accusing that woman were adulterers."

Oscar: "It seems there were great oppressions at that time, right? And one of them was that a woman was treated like dirt, because if she, the female, did it, it was terrible; if the man did it they didn't even notice."

Olivia: "It was the machismo of that time, which was very strong, but we go right on having it in our time. That woman didn't commit adultery all by herself, and the man she committed adultery with, they didn't accuse him."

Oscar: "Yes, they didn't bring him."[3]

Oscar certainly is well disposed, but Teresita and Olivia seem to sharpen his appreciation of how long machismo has been twising the lives of women.

· CELEBRATING ·

Christian ministry ought to be thoroughly servant, indeed, and fully concerned with proclaiming the justice that the gospel of Christ demands. But it should also express the joy of Christ and the peace of the Christ's Spirit. It should, in other words, bring home to people the goodness of the news it carries. Certainly the faces and voices of all Christians, but especially those in orders, can convey an evangelical joy and peace. Certainly a hopeful theology and ethics, spelling out what the grace of God can do to untangle twisted personalities or social situations, is a blessing greatly to be desired. Yet the most dramatic communication of the goodness of the Christian news occurs in neither of these modalities. The most dramatic communication occurs in the Christian eucharist, where Jesus' followers celebrate the messianic banquet that their faith in his resurrection warrants.

As is well known, both Jesus and the Judaism of his time loved to picture the Kingdom of God, or the time when God would make human affairs right, as a time of partying. Their sense in relying on this imagery was that where two or three gather in God's name they find the fullest joy. In the parable of the prodigal son (Luke 15:11–32), the father spontaneously expresses his joy at getting back his wastrel son by throwing a party: "'Bring quickly the best robe, and put it on him; and put a ring on his hand, and shoes on his feet; and bring the fatted calf and kill it, and let us eat and make merry'" (15:22–23). The father clearly stands for Jesus' heavenly Father, ever gracious and forgiving. The prodigal son stands for our sinful selves, who again and again are both ingrates and spiritual wanderers. Less noted, perhaps, but ultimately equally interesting is the elder brother who resents the party being thrown for the returned prodigal. Rightly has he come to stand for the dutiful religious types who fulfill their responsibilities exactly but have little fund of good will to spend upon either sinners or penitents. The words of the father to him are both kindly and instructive: "'Son, you are always with me, and all that is mine is yours. It was fitting to make merry and be glad, for this your brother was dead, and is alive; he was lost, and is found'" (15:31-32).

In numerous other parables we catch echoes of the same message: God is more generous than any rigorous human calculi can imagine. For God, the slightest human show of good will is provocation to give a reward or throw a party. There is no implication in this that God is a trivial sort of ultimate reality, only concerned in a divine way to eat, drink, and make merry. For on no tomorrow does God die, and in no today does God need outside things to fill up the measure of the divine contentedness. The figure of the vineyard owner who rewards the laborers who came at the end of the day (Matthew 20:1-16), like the figure of the father of the prodigal son, suggests a God at least as superior to us morally as ontologically. In Johannine terms, God so loved the world he gave the only begotten Son for the world's salvation. In Pauline terms, while we were still sinners God loved us, and nothing can separate us from the love of God in Christ Jesus our Lord.

The Christian eucharist or Lord's Supper ritualizes a communal response to the divine largess. Certainly it also recalls the sorrows of the farewell meal that Jesus shared with his friends before his death, and therefore moves in the framework of the Jewish passover. But it keeps the overtones of the messianic banquet and the love feast that the early Christians composed. It reminds the world, by first reminding Christians themselves, that God's wisdom is wiser than that of the worldly pundits (who regularly offer the counsel that it is necessary for one or more people to die to preserve the status quo). It repeats the key Christian conviction that by dying Christ destroyed our death and by rising he restored our life. *Christus Victor*, as much of the patristic soteriology considered Jesus, took Satan to the mat and broke his back. No longer need we fear "the enemy of our human nature," as Ignatius Loyola called him. At each eucharist we can celebrate our liberation from the worst sorts of bondage: moral impotence, meaninglessness, condemnation to a law of the jungle, frustration in a noisy time ended only by a silent death.

What is there especially for women to celebrate? In Christian perspective, there is the demise of the cultural bias that has frequently lumped women with children and the insane as people not eligible to give witness in court, to take part in the councils of civil rulers, or to mediate between human beings and divinity at the altar. There is the affirmation of the love, the peace-making, the reconciling of enemies, and the nourishing of both faith and community life that women have historically served more fully than men. Because the message of Jesus goes to the rotten roots of cultural systems that would discriminate against any human being, thus leveling all human beings as debtors to God's grace, women can take to heart countercultural symbols that make them as much children of God as are their sons and brothers. No doubt that was the reason so many women committed themselves to the historical Jesus, remaining more faithful than most of the male apostles in seeing things through to the apparent defeat of Calvary. No doubt that is the liberating possibility so many women glimpse today, and why today women are the majority of just about every denomination's membership.

The liberation that Catholic Christian women find in the gospel of Christ is not vitiated by this tradition's second-class treatment of them, but it is both restrained and radicalized. One has to feel restrained and saddened when the egalitarianism of the gospel is contradicted by the sexism of one's ecclesiastical institutions, although of course the shame falls completely on the institutional side. Mature women hardly delight in seeing their imperial male leaders revealed by the gospel to have no clothes, but they may be forgiven a smile or two. And these smiles fold into Catholic Christian women's long radicalization, even when many of the women themselves do not fully realize it. For in church matters as much as in secular matters, Catholic women continue to play out the scenario of being both the strongest emotional supporters and the most devastatingly thorough debunkers. Just as they don't know whether to cry or to laugh when they encounter a pompous military type from the Pentagon, so they don't know whether to cry or to laugh when a rigid clerical type freaks out at the mention of women's liberation. Because they are at the margins of the ideologico-symbolic structures that have been thrown up to legitimate male arrogation of church power, women are less likely to accept them uncritically, are more likely instinctively to have demythologized them. Whether by conditioning or a certain grace that may flow through estrogen, Catholic Christian women tend to pay the pomp and circumstance of hierarchical power little heed, realizing that their only hope of salvation lies in something much realer and less fragile than such pathetic princedom.

So it is liberation from the sinfulness or obtuseness of the church, as well as from the depredations of general cultural biases, that women celebrate at the eucharist. They certainly should not neglect their own sins, which often tend to stem from underdevelopment and timidity, and they certainly should not avert their eyes from the objective evils that the sexual imbalances of Catholic Christianity have caused. It should continue to embarrass and anger them that their tradition seems fixated on sexuality, always popping off about abortion or birth control or homosexuality or fornication. It should gladden their hearts that recent episcopal statements have shown more interest in peacemaking and economic justice. Yet, contrary to quite a few Catholic feminists, I do not find these socio-systemic foci of liberation the true center of the eucharist celebration. To my mind the ultimate cause for joy is the unthinkable fact that the deepest mystery has shown itself an unconditionally loving parent, no more able to abandon us, whatever circumstances we fall into, than a nursing mother can abandon her child. (We must make a note to recall this depth of the eucharistic celebration when it comes to truly Christian attitudes toward the victims of abortion. Though the church has felt it necessary to consider abortion cause for ipso facto excommunication, we can believe that God has never abandoned any woman forced into such extremis.)

· HEALING ·

The last topic that I have chosen to preface this orientational reflection on Christian ministry is healing, another work traditionally congenial to women. For although the sacramental healing mediated through penance has been reserved to the male clergy, Catholic Christianity certainly has raised up myriads of women who have been very effective healers of both bodies and spirits. As has been true in our other considerations, the argument I find obvious in such a fact is the aptness or suitability of many women for official church leadership and priestly ministry. However, let me not beat this drum once again so much as explore the beauty and pervasive significance latent in Christian healing.

The example we have from Jesus, in the New Testament, coming as it does from a more holistic time and culture, treats healing as a psychosomatic unity. When Jesus forgives people their sins, he works spiritual changes that lead to good physical effects. When he heals withered limbs or gives sight to eyes previously darkened, he either enjoins the beneficiary to go and sin no more or he refers to the God by whose power he has been able to make such a benefaction. From time to time Jesus refers to seizures or physical infirmities as marks of the bondage of Satan. In healing either bodies or spirits, he therefore is about the work of liberation. We do well, it follows, not to pay excess attention to the distinctions among liberation, healing, and salvation that theologians sometimes advance. The variety of words and concepts used simply suggests that the New Testament authors found that the good effects of Jesus' ministry scattered like so many seeds of one vigorous sowing.

The salvation that Christ brought, as the etymology of the word implies, was a restoration to health (*salus*). The justification or righteousness over which the Protestant reformers spilled so much ink boils down to restoring the relation between human beings and God to health. The problem had never lain on God's side, of course, all the references to the divine "wrath" notwithstanding. To portray God as a vindictive tyrant, or even as a jurist bound by the sublimity of legal justice to exact full satisfaction for honor lost, is to forget completely the father of the prodigal son. God hardly needs human recognition or praise to make the divine existence heavenly (although Alice Walker uses quite effectively the notion that God creates beauty to solicit admiration[4]). The healing that grace imparts wholly targets the human recipient. If the farthest reaches of that grace are what the Catholic tradition called "elevating" (taking people up into the divine nature, divinizing them), it remains true that the restorative effects of grace (*gratia sanans*) also are great cause for joy.

Today it is the systemic implications of divine healing that most intrigue liberation theologians, rather than the implications that seem to seize the attention of the healers who dominate the electronic church. The healing that Christian ministry best serves is the restoration of the human community's abilities to sustain progress or development. Where societies break down because of darkened minds and weakened wills, the grace of God, somewhat specified in the theological virtues of faith, hope, and charity, offers powers that can heal the sickness at the root of social dysfunctions and open again the prospect of a decent earthly existence.

Bernard Lonergan is skilled at working out this analysis of how the gracious powers of salvation are the most practical aids Christians can bring to disjointed economics and politics. In the final analysis the problems we now suffer, like the problems that past generations and cultures have suffered, are due more to human disorder than to natural disasters or deficiencies. Because we so easily miss the balance between time and eternity, God and our neighbors, love and justice, and the so many other seeming contraries, we fail to distribute the goods of the earth as a generous and provident Creator would want. We fail to honor the radical equality of all human beings, regardless of race or sex, as a parental God who makes the sun shine and the rain fall on just and unjust alike would want. We pervert the proper hierarchy of values, preferring material and perishable goods to spiritual goods that partake of heaven right now. We lay waste to the land we ought to serve as stewards and pay posterity virtually no heed. Who can deliver us from this thoroughgoing disorder and bondage? Nothing but the healing that God has revealed through Jesus Christ (but has actually offered and somewhat achieved in all times and places: God is never without witness to the saving power of the creative mystery).

Christian ministry, of course, serves this healing grace. It does not produce it as something of human doing for which the ministers themselves can claim credit. When Christian ministers serve the gospel and practical programs of healing, they must still account themselves unprofitable servants, people who have only done what God says we all should be doing. At best they plant and water, waiting and praying for an increase that only God can give. And this is not at all hyperbolic, especially when the context is economics or politics. The changes of heart necessary to convert an unjust economy into one that meets the canons of distributive fairness, or needed to change a political system so that the numerical majority of the people are not left on the margins as nonparticipants—such changes go far below what human prudence or eloquence can expect to create. People are only healed into a decent humanity, only lose their grasping selfishness and have the scales drop from their eyes, when special pain or special joy forces them out of business as usual and, in effect, produces a conversion. The ultimate healing of which the gospel speaks is that which makes it possible for whole people to give God whole minds, hearts, souls, and strengths. True salvation starts to take hold in a society when a significant fraction of the population really does love its neighbors as itself.

I need not belabor the point, I hope, that this inner spirituality means little, or at least is highly suspect, unless it finds issue in behavioral or political changes. The Catholic tradition has been wise to insist that faith and works have an integral connection. And I feel I need not apologize for pointing out that healing today has some distinctively feminist overtones, both because women have nursed so much of human illness and because the church, considered as a sacramental community of healing, has sores and fractures of its own to cure. With the raising of women's consciousness of their pervasive mistreatment and alienation from equality with men has come a deep sense of victimization. The brutal form manifest in rape and spousal abuse rightly gets the headlines, but beneath this surface lies a violence and suffering that is frighteningly pervasive.

For Christian ministers the roots of this violence are a sinful revolt against God, who alone might be said to have the authority to wreck any creature, and who instructively chooses to be long-suffering and merciful. It is certainly true that those who perpetrate violence often suffer from woeful insecurities themselves. It is also true that these insecurities argue more for women's advancement to full equality with men in all of society's rights and duties than for any backing away from women's liberation. The roots of the insecurities about which one can best be compassionate are the undeniable better instincts of the people pretending to hurtful authority. In their bones, they know that they are radically equal to their victims in humanity, that God has not made them little kings. No honest or intelligent spirit can long support abusive patriarchy today, so those who cannot face the changes that honesty would compel have to twist both the truth and themselves, often becoming spiritually, mentally, and physically ill. The grace that heals, it follows, is bound to wield the scalpel of spiritual light or truth. The discriminations that claim sanction from a God who is light in whom there is no darkness at all ring false from their first voicing.

·3·

WOMEN'S WORK

· MOTHERHOOD ·

Women perform innumerable ministerial works in the Christian church, so the formal ordination denied women in Catholic Christianity runs counter to many actual realities. The women who serve the love of Christ as teachers, counselors, nurses, and even sacramental adjutants all argue, by their simple being, that denying people official orders because they are of female sex certainly is suspect and probably is simply irrational. The arguments suggested by women's advancement in medicine, higher education, government, and other realms of leadership run to the same conclusion. Is the Christian priesthood so peculiar a realm that having female chromosomes should be a disqualification? Does the grace of God anoint with the charismata of sacramental leadership only those who produce testosterone? The socio-cultural arguments against the possibility of women's effective religious leadership have manifestly failed, so we are left with only these pseudo-biological prejudices. They hardly seem worthy of serious religious consideration.

What does seem quite worthy of serious religious consideration is the evolutionary work that nature has given women. The two hitherto irreducible tasks that sexual differentiation has imposed are motherhood and fatherhood. True enough, in our day "parenthood" rightly covers the vast majority of tasks implied in child rearing, since such tasks are not sexually determined. It remains true, however, that women are the ones who carry new life within them, nurse new life with the substance of their own bodies, and in most cultures dominate the early years of children's formation. Without prejudice to men's current or future roles in child rearing, let us reflect on the attitudes and skills that motherhood has virtually ordained that women would develop. If we find that they are more consonant with the ideals of the Christian priesthood than inimical, we shall have another basis for challenging the discrimination that Catholic Christianity continues to practice.

The biblical figure that God can no more abandon any human being than a nursing mother could abandon her child epitomizes the scriptural sense of the divine love. In consort with other imagery, the passages in the prophets where God is moved to the divine center or womb like a woman arrested to her core show that even so highly patriarchal a culture as biblical Israel sensed that maternal love gives strong hints of the divine passion. Jesus spoke mainly of his Father, but he balanced the figure of the shepherd seeking out the single lost sheep with the figure of the woman sweeping her house for the single lost coin. The love of God obviously goes beyond our sexual stereotypes, being validly prefigured in any human care that is faithful and creative. If biblical Judaism, which has been the matrix of all Christian theology, shied away from feminine imagery, both because of the patriarchal slant of its own culture and because of its reservations about the sexual component of the neighboring Canaanite religion that focused on fertility, it nevertheless never cast a veto against the divine transcendence of its own biases. God must always be greater than our faltering impressions of the divine nature. Whatever seems ultimately good, creative, or restorative deserves serious theological consideration.

So, although it is true that biblical religion did not sanction the androgynous depictions of divinity that developed in other traditions such as Hinduism, it is false to say that Christian theology—in the strict sense of the "Christian understanding of God"—is misogynistic. When it comes to the ultimate mystery of the love that makes creation and overcomes sin, the ways of men have no symbolic superiority. The joys and griefs of women are every bit as useful.

Mothers, then, move as clearly in the wake of the divine parenthood as do fathers. The symbiosis of pregnancy, in fact, has few equals from the range of masculine experience in suggesting the intimacy of the divine-human relationship. Where classical Christian metaphysics described creation as ongoing, since without the divine grant of existence moment by moment contingent beings

would fall back into nothingness, today's theologian might spontaneously picture a divine pregnancy. The picture would falter in
many ways, of course, since there is no term to the divine "conser-
vation" that keeps all creatures in being. But it suggests something
of the common life that God the source shares with us the recipients.
As the fetus depends on the mother's whole biological system, so we
creatures depend on the Creator's whole necessity of being. As the
relationship with the child colors the mother's full range of concerns,
so the relationship with creation, by God's free choice, makes the
divine existence different than it need have been.

And since the concerns of the revealed, biblical God run more in
the direction of life and healing than in the direction of existence or
being, the emotional side of motherhood offers another whole set of
useful analogies. Granted the proper purification of their anthropo-
morphism, we can say that God hopes for the flourishing of human
beings the way that a mother hopes for the flourishing of the life she
is carrying. The sacrifices that pregnant women make, like the
sacrifices that mothers make long after their children have gained
independent existence, shed great light on the selfless character of
the divine agape. Using them to deepen and broaden our perspective, we can reread the indications of God's selfless generosity to
greater effect. And then the mother of the prodigal son, missing in
Luke's lovely story, can step forth imaginatively to complete the
analogy Luke's Christ intended. Her concern for the ne'er-do-well
would not differ substantially from that of the loving father, but it
would have if anything sharper or more persuasive overtones. For
she, after all, would have carried the boy as flesh of her flesh for
nine months. His first needs, smiles, and steps would have received
her rapt attention. So she, at least as well as the generous father,
would have had a stake in his movement from careless hurtfulness
to humbled return. Her posture of never-failing, unconditional
love would have been at least as convincing as the father's, and so at
least as good a cipher for the divine attitude.

My object is not to rewrite the New Testament, nor gloss over the
complexity in any symbolization of the divine love, especially that
being created in a highly self-conscious time like our own. We know
that mothers and children have tangled relationships, just as fathers
and children do. We know that mothers' traditional dominance of
child rearing has made their parenthood more ambiguous than that

of fathers: mothers are both more elevated as paragons of idealistic love and more resented as images of a life that promised total satisfaction and could never deliver. So importing motherhood into theology proper, or even into the symbolic foundations of the Christian priesthood, would be a complicated task. But only our habituation to the correspondingly masculine side of theology and the foundations of priesthood keeps us from realizing that the same dynamics have always played there. That God should be prayed to as "Father," or that Catholic priests should be addressed as "Father," is no more natural or contrived than the use of "Mother" would have been. We can't leap outside the history that serves us as our cultural skin, but we can become critical and honest enough to realize the quotient of accident or arbitrariness that plays in all theologies or symbol systems. We can accept the implications of cultural relativity, link them with the demands of liberation in our time, and stop using a contingent history to buttress discrimination against women. The "natural," biologically given work of women to keep the human species going is as valid a basis for depicting the divine Creator as is the natural, biologically given work of men. The motherhood at which women have toiled is as honest and useful a basis for conceiving the Christian priesthood as is the fatherhood at which men have toiled.

· TEACHING ·

When anthropologists discuss sexual differentiation they frequently drop into a long-playing discussion about the relations between "nature" and "culture." In studying the self-conception of numerous societies, they find a bias that associates women with nature and men with culture. This bias, of course, cannot be separated from the distribution of tasks and power in the given society, so it turns out that most of the societies in which women are associated more closely with nature than are men have a patriarchal slant. If culture is preferred to nature—thought of as higher and more prestigious—then it makes sense for male leaders of a patriarchal society to take culture as their proper domain. In that case women's cyclical bodily clock, their more obvious role in reproduction, and their perhaps more holistic sense of the body-mind relationship associate them with nature, somewhat to their discredit. Men may agree to women's control of the early years of children's education, when teaching runs together with filling hungry mouths and wiping dirty bottoms, but they think "higher" education should be a masculine preserve since it deals with the traditions and lore they find crucial to preserving the tribe's identity. Men then develop a cluster of symbols that promote the notion of their rationality, decisiveness, and talent for demanding leadership. Women, by contrast, are relegated to the domestic sphere and are said to naturally be followers.

In reality, of course, nothing in this sketch holds up, for the interactions between nature and culture are notoriously subtle and mold women as complicatedly as they mold men. The myths of many cultures associate the coming of culture with women, and the theologies of androgynous religious cultures such as Hinduism often make a goddess the patroness of music or learning. Prehistorians tend to the opinion that women are more likely to have invented agriculture than men, while students of child development think that the first three or five years are the most crucial "education" that any human being receives. The role-modeling, instruction, encouragement, disciplining, and overall care that women provide the tribe is as essential as what men do. The wisdom that women accumulate and pass on, even in societies professedly patriarchal, probably shapes as much of what people actually depend upon as does the wisdom of men.

All of which is simply to say that there is no sound basis for thinking that the responsibility of the Christian ministry to teach the faith, preserve solid doctrine, make catechetical applications, and generally illumine the always mysterious divine reality carries anything specifically masculine about it. As the progress women have made in higher education in the past generation suggests, when cultural stereotypes are challenged and sexist barriers fall, women prove quite as successful at teaching as men. In fact, the greater personalism that women have tended to develop in recent Western culture serves them well as formal instructors. On the whole, they are more successful teachers than men, because on the whole they better communicate the interest in students and sense of where students are on which good teaching depends. I don't mean this description as a positive stereotype, let alone an invariant pattern. It is simply one professional educator's personal observation.

Nonetheless, it inclines me to impatience with roadblocks set in the way of women's exercising an official, ordained teaching role in Catholic Christianity, just as I am impatient with the hindrances women suffer when they try to exercise other aspects of the formal Christian ministry. To teach well one has to know both the subject matter to be communicated and the two poles of the process of inter-personal communication, the self of the teacher and the self of the learner. Men may have the prejudice that they are naturally more talented at the objective mastery of such bodies of information as traditional Christian theology, although the grades of graduate students in theology do not support this prejudice. Women may believe that they are naturally more skilled at interpersonal communication. This is also a prejudice, but both psychological studies and intelligent observation tend to support it. Common sense therefore promotes the opinion that candidates for the Christian ministry of teaching sacred doctrine should be evaluated in terms of their scholarly, pastoral, and pedagogical aptitudes—and nothing else. (I am not denying that it would be wise to require certain standards of moral behavior, but in a properly Christian perspective those bear no sexual prejudice. Certainly there is no basis in Jesus' teaching for asserting that women are less competent in morality than men, and certainly the historical record does not list women as the great slaughterers and wreckers.)

But how has women's teaching worked out through the centuries? What are the principal values and pedagogical accents that we associate with female teachers, from the nursery and grammar school through the other places where women give instruction? This is too broad a question to admit of apodictic answers, yet perhaps a generalist may be excused for trying to suggest a few tendencies. On the whole, I find that women promote an ethics distinctive for care and use a pedagogy distinctively dialogical. The ethics of care is related to the dialogical pedagogy in that women regularly commit themselves to the maintenance of relationships. Thus in Carol Gilligan's well known study of feminine moral development one sees pre-teenage girls preferring to stop the game rather than create alienated winners and losers.[1] We see the young women rejecting the assumptions of Kohlberg's famous dilemma of Heinz, the man who must either steal a drug his wife needs or let her die. They sense that this is an incomplete, if not indeed invalid way to structure any moral situation, and their instinctive way out is to want to get all the parties involved talking, so that by cooperating, giving and taking, they can resolve things to everyone's satisfaction. The primary value in many of these considerations is a justice that very prominently takes into account people's feelings. Where boys of comparable age tend to make rights and duties the ethical key, girls sketch a holistic ethics in which not giving pain is at least equally important.

Now, is an ethics powered by care and a pedagogy focused by dialogue (clarification through ongoing conversation) congenial to handing on and clarifying the gospel? Or does the teaching proper to Christian ministry necessitate a more dispassionate moral sensibility and a more authoritarian pedagogy? Perhaps there is room for a difference of opinion but my conviction is that, at the very least, the teaching proper to Christian ministry needs a strong dose of care and dialogue. At the most, one might argue that when care does not predominate over dispassion and dialogue does not predominate over authoritarianism, the teaching proper to Christian ministry is in bad shape. I will not say that the catechetical problems of Catholic Christianity in the past few centuries have all stemmed from a stereotypically masculine dispassion and authoritarianism, but I will say that the all male power structure and the generally impersonal cast of the catechetical model that prevailed until Vatican II suggest a suspiciously close connection. By contrast, the newer catechetical models, which stress sharing the story by which Christians have lived, come closer to the ways that feminists tend to teach and do business.[2] They are personalist, making individual human beings more important than laws, and the love that they find at the center of the gospel has a high quotient of care. When they draw on the biblical symbol of the covenant that God struck with Israel, they make ongoing dialogue the heart of Christian pedagogy. The laws associated with Sinai were no more important than the covenant bond they were to express and promote. Similarly, the "letters" of Christian doctrine and ethics were less important than the Spirit of love, personal and caring, at the heart of the new covenant.

· NURSING ·

We have been speaking of women's work, stressing the ways that women's roles in bringing forth new life and clarifying people's

minds (especially the minds of children) seem congenial to Christian ministry. Christianity speaks insistently of a new life brought
by Christ and the Spirit. It has a passion to bring the light and wisdom of this life to all people, whom it firmly believes God summons
to a covenantal dialogue. Our third topic, nursing, involves the
nurture of new life and the healing of life that has been wounded or
sickened. In imagery developed by Julian of Norwich, a medieval
anchorite, Jesus is portrayed as a mother who nurses the faith and
love of her believers. In imagery sped through the news wires because of the work of Mother Teresa of Calcutta, the ministry of
healing the poorest of the poor is one of the most powerful suggestions of Christ's meaning for today's world.

Nursing in the sense of feeding conjures up the action of the Spirit
in our depths. The Holy Spirit is the person of the Trinity most often
given a feminine persona by Christian tradition, and a frequent
counsel in writings about contemplative prayer is that one should
abide with what gives nourishment. The person who prays regularly, the classical treatises say, moves beyond the simply petitionary sort of dialogue that dominates the beginner. He or she also
moves beyond the meditation that is concerned with getting clear
the main notions of the Christian world view. In contemplative
prayer a certain simplicity develops such that the main work is
nourishing the person's hunger for God, facilitating the being-to-
being or heart-to-heart flow of love that is unsatisfied by just
words or ideas. Like a child nursing at the breast, the traditional
contemplative learned to repose on the divine silence and open
herself to the Holy Spirit. At the end of the regular session of
prayer the "gain" was not so much new ideas or firmer resolve.
The gain was restored peace and joy, renewed faith and love. The
contemplative came to depend on prayer the way he depended on
breakfast, lunch, and dinner.

The second connotation of nursing, in which the agent of
religion helps to heal breaks and bruises, is perhaps less distinctively feminine than the connotation of breast-feeding, but it too
strongly suggests that women have a solid endowment of talent for
priestly healing. For if men have until recently dominated the
medical profession in modern Western societies, women have
dominated the nursing profession. And in non-Western societies as
well as in the premodern world at large, women have functioned

prominently as healers, often using their knowledge of herbs and their sensitivity to spiritual influences to fine therapeutic effect.

The healing now most often associated with ordination to Christian ministry is reconciliation to God and neighbor. Where sin cuts the offender off from peaceful relations with the Creator, the ministry of reconciliation that Catholic Christianity has focused in the sacrament of penance restores the bond. Where sin divides communities or sets friend against friend, the sacrament of penance has ritualized both the internal changes of heart needed for a new beginning and the resolve to extend a word of apology or a hand of renewed affection. People have to forgive themselves, also, and be helped to heal the self-doubt or even self-hatred that can come to corrode their souls. They have to learn to look on nature, the church, their hometown, and just about everything else in their world as a fit object for their care and helpfulness. So healing, which at the foundational level is little different from feminist care, becomes part and parcel of a reverence for life and a respect for all creation. It stems from the benevolence poured forth in our hearts by the Holy Spirit. It wants to imitate Christ in giving sight and restoring hope.

Do women now work at healing of this sort? In the typical household, office, hospital, school, or neighborhood do they shoulder much of the work of reknitting torn relationships, consoling those who mourn? Of course they do. Men do good work in these areas, to be sure, but women at least carry their load. The stereotype that women's interpersonal sensitivity overheats their interactions and actually produces considerable hurt and taking offense has its bases. In the healthier society that a liberated set of possibilities for both sexes would produce we no doubt would find less cattiness and oversensitivity. Even granting the quanta of useless sufferings that women cause, however, it remains true that they regularly seek out those who are troubled, regularly make the little gesture or say the small word that makes the day pleasanter. Women have had less say in the competitive economy and war making which cause the greater sufferings of our time. There have been far fewer women murderers, rapists, thieves, and other perpetrators of criminal hurt. This in itself, of course, is no canonization, but it does suggest that a penchant for not giving hurt is simply the other side of a desire to nurse to health and prosperity.

The image of the church latent in a Christian ministry concerned with healing deserves serious consideration. If the Christian community is to be a band of servant disciples, rather than a band of people who possess the truth and with it the mandate to pontificate, it must make the needs of the suffering more significant than its own privileges. Indeed, it must make the needs of the suffering more significant than its own sense of propriety or its own image in the community at large. Just as Jesus did not worry that he was consorting with the wrong sort of people, those whom his society considered degenerate and polluting, so the church should not worry that its ministry is not sitting well with the high and mighty of its time. Jesus saw himself as sent to those who had greatest need of a physician. Those who were prospering had only second call upon him. Again and again the church has forgotten this lesson, tending to save the saved and consort with the respectable. Indeed, at many times and places respectability was thought to coincide with Christian virtue, or even with Christian sanctity. When it turned out that respectability, in the sense of a vigorous and successful share in the status quo, was a central part of the problem, the church came into a crisis of conscience.

A good example of the current crisis of conscience set for the church by a theology that would stress healing and liberation is the sanctions that Roman curial officials have leveled against Latin American theologians such as Leonardo Boff. Boff has received the strongest punishment (silencing), because he has written the strongest liberational critiques of the church itself.[3] But Küng and Schillebeeckx have been called on the carpet for similar views, while Gustavo Gutierrez, the father of Latin American liberation theology, is ever in danger of being penalized. The official Catholicism of our day lags so far behind the best instincts of the liberationists that it cannot hear their call to repentance as anything applying to itself. So the encyclicals of Pope John Paul II say wonderful things about social justice and peacemaking to the outside world, while within the church justice, peace, and liberation lag behind. The bugbear the Roman Curia finds with the Latin American liberation theologians is their insistence that vigorous Christian faith means taking sides, being political, whether one is priest or peasant.

The bugbear I find with the institutional Catholic church is the enslavement of half the population in second-class status, the increasingly grievous wounds to women's faith. I have been saddened though not surprised to find at recent national meetings that the female Catholic intelligentsia has just about written off the official hierarchy. Rome's intransigent opposition to women's liberation to full equality with men within the church has come to symbolize a deafness or inauthenticity that most Catholic intellectuals don't expect to change in their lifetime. As a result, they qualify their Catholicism to a love of a beautiful and rich tradition, thinking that the institutional Catholicism now dominating most parishes more hinders than helps the tradition. As a result, the future Christian ministry has a great deal of healing to accomplish among Catholic women.

· PRAYING ·

The Christian liturgy has been traditionally understood to be the major work of God's people, and even though women have not been allowed formal leadership of the Catholic Christian liturgy, they certainly have contributed a fair share to this popular work. From the old ladies in black shawls who have populated the dark and quiet churches to the hundreds of convents of cloistered nuns, women have sent toward heaven a constant stream of adoration and petition. Both at the formal sacramental liturgy and at their stations for private prayer, they have assured that the otherworldly, gratuitous dimension of Christianity would stay properly potent.

I will not debate the propriety of otherworldly prayer, for it seems to me obvious, from both the historical record of Christian faith and from any religious analysis of human existence, that God is always more than the sum of our concerns. When God does not have a surplus dimension, or is not mysterious in the proper sense of being a fullness we could never exhaust, we have no genuine divinity who could create the world from nothingness simply by letting its inmost love take outer, delimited form. The basis for a contemplative prayer essentially concerned with glorifying God in the spirit of the *Gloria* of the Mass or of the *Te Deum* is precisely this divine transcendence, and one can argue that "humanity," being correlative to the widest outreach of our spirit or heart, shrinks destructively when God is not radically transcendent.

This said, however, I want to spend the remainder of this section reflecting on the decidedly this-worldly function that women's laborious prayer has fulfilled throughout the centuries. For, like the widow before the unjust judge, women have regularly almost assaulted the divine silence, forcing it to attend to human miseries and in the process daring God to default on the contract implicit in the human impulse to petition the ultimate. Luke's parable is worth recalling: "And he told them a parable, to the effect that they ought always to pray and not lose heart. He said, 'In a certain city there was a judge who neither feared God nor regarded man; and there was a widow in that city who kept coming to him and saying, "Vindicate me against my adversary." For a while he refused; but afterward he said to himself, "Though I neither fear God nor regard man, yet because this widow bothers me, I will vindicate her, or she will wear me out by her continual coming."' And the Lord said, 'Hear what the unrighteous judge says. And will not God vindicate his elect, who cry to him day and night? Will he delay long over them? I tell you, he will vindicate them speedily. Nevertheless, when the Son of man comes, will he find faith on earth?'" (Luke 18:1–8)

The thematic sentence says that Christians ought always to pray and not lose heart. There is a stubbornness at the core of the Christian profession of faith, an insistence that one day becomes a blank check. The believer signs the check over to God, saying that nothing can separate her from God's love and that she will not tolerate God's absence from any dimension of her life. If God is what God is supposed to be, God has to care about everything that she cares for. One could say, then, that the believer, in pushing her blank check across the divider, asks God to issue a blank check in return. The transaction goes forward in the coin of trust, and it must aim at a certain equality. The believer knows that she is asked to accept all the things she cannot change, interpreting them as God's providence. But she also knows that she has the right, probably even the duty to nag at God when that providence seems destructive or careless. So in midnight vigils at the beds of their sick children mothers have regularly told God that the situation was intolerable. No doubt they have kept a small corner swept clear of anger and prepared for resignation, but their first concern has been to get God to change the present evil state of affairs.

This nagging persistence is solidly founded in Jewish religion. Abraham haggles with God and Job insists on justice. The biblical

God is portrayed as interactive, covenanted, defined not as our philosophical schemata deduce but as time shows the divine nature to be. If the Exodus is the central paradigm from the Hebrew Bible, then God shows in Israelite time that divinity is concerned about liberation. If the death and resurrection of Jesus is the central paradigm of the New Testament, then God has liberations in store that we can barely conceive. The mutual testing that petitionary prayer sponsors is probably the most existential and rigorous assay of faith. If we badger the divine silence, insisting that a real God would make a difference, we put most of our chips on the line. As well, we insert ourselves into a process that may radically change us, for we may emerge either as warranted atheists, convinced that the silence is only uncaring dust, or as people humbled on the model of Job, forced to confess that the ultimate shape of justice is beyond our competence.

Once again, I would not claim that women have had any monopoly on this testing process, but I would claim that they have stood out for making their faith concrete. If only because so frequently throughout history women have felt that society gave them little justice or recourse, women regularly have sought contact with more ultimate powers. The women who stood by Jesus to his bitter end on the cross probably were moved more by their personal love for him than by the hoping against hope that petitionary prayer can bring into view, but in fact they were the portion of the early followers who stood out for defying worldly expectations—for stubbornly standing before God and demanding justice. The evangelists seem instinctively to appreciate this signal quality of the women's faith for they agree in making Mary Magdalene the first witness of the resurrection. As though God were rewarding those who best hoped against hope or best defied the more prudential calculi of the less unreservedly loving, the Christ first speaks to Mary, and she responds as the Good Shepherd predicted (John 10:4), knowing his voice because she belongs to him.[4]

At any rate, the dimensions of discipleship and ministry laid bare by persistent, ultimately self-abandoning petitionary prayer seem to me profound indeed, and I think it only fair to indicate women's historically large share in them. If the Christian ministry has succeeded in making credible the idea that God does care about human beings and will "vindicate them speedily," women deserve much of the credit. The women who come to Jesus to beg cures of their children simply prefigure the generations of women who asked God to make a difference in their hard lives and came away from their prayers convinced that they had been answered. We may often have good reasons for thinking this prayer showed superstition or a lack of theological sophistication. God seems less chary than we, probably because God is less concerned about superstition than about love. I see women's prayer as finally a great expression of women's religious love. They have hated the evils and sufferings of their times and asked God to change things. They have loved God not only for the changes they felt they experienced but for the barer fact that "God" gave them reason to hope that change might be possible at all. Since I think that conveying this hope is quintessential to proclaiming the good news of Christ, I think women's inclination to petitionary prayer and their historical competence at it make them wonderfully apt for orders. Once again, therefore, I find the religious work that women actually have accomplished contradicting Catholic Christianity's veto of their suitability for orders, and once again Catholic Christianity is the loser in the showdown.

·4·

WOMEN'S LEADERSHIP

· CARE ·

Having considered some of the key ingredients of both Christian ministry and women's historical work, we now turn to women's leadership. This leadership, of course, cannot be completely separated from either Christian ministry or women's work. Women have actually ministered greatly for the Christian faith throughout history, even though often not eligible for formal orders, and women's work has frequently been that of leading the domestic or local community of faith by example, stimulus, or outright taking charge. My main interest in this chapter, as in the previous one, is the distinctive way that women have exercised their authority. For while certainly the leadership of women has shared many traits with the leadership of men, it has also instinctively followed its own counsel and developed traits less prominent in the leadership of men.

The first of these traits, already noted when we considered women's nursing, is care. The leadership of women regularly expresses itself as care for the group being led. This in itself does not distinguish female leaders from male, but it sets up the distinctive emotional charge that women's leadership is apt to carry, and it reminds us of the dialogical way of trying to produce change that reigns in women's circles. Men care for their groups and are often deeply involved in the business or religious projects they are heading, but their conditioning has been not to let this care show as tenderness or any other "emotional" attachment or commitment. They have been permitted, by the amorphous sanctioners of our social patterns, to get angry when their leadership has been frustrated but not to weep out of disappointment and hurt. For models they have been shown stoic generals and crisp executives, not the Christ who wept over Jerusalem and would have gathered its people the way a hen gathers her chicks under her wings. So the stereotypical care of men for the works and people they have led has not had the intimacy or person-alism or vulnerability of feminine leadership. Its flow charts and paradigms have run to a hierarchalism that insulated leaders from the emotional effects their actions created in both themselves and their followers. Women, by contrast, have tended to set the chairs in a circle and share both the power and the aftermath more demo-cratically. The leader has usually felt a major responsibility to keep up her charges' morale, and the charges have been led by their emotional involvement to respond to their head as a matter of per-sonal relationship rather than job description.

I realize, of course, that this sketch is impressionistic, but I mean it mainly as a base from which to launch a reflection on care itself. Again and again, the antidote to the pathologies and dysfunctions being strewn by our bureaucratization seems to lie in the more per-sonal energies of care. Again and again, the way back to efficiency and worker satisfaction sets out from a home base of care. In just the few years that I have been writing books, I have seen two of my best editors quit because the care that previously had prevailed in their companies was declining before management experts and in-creased computerization. The result was often that a book that used to take nine months to produce now took a full year. Questions posed to editors that used to get relatively quick attention now dissolved into indecisiveness and inefficient correspondence. It may be sim-plistic to see this trend as anti-feminist, but I think the hypothesis deserves consideration. The current trend certainly often seems care-less, compared to the prior ideals, and people are often being subordinated to profits in a way that demonstrates the feminist link with a radically Christian critique of capitalism.

I have only a small toehold in publishing, so perhaps leadership in educational institutions would be a better example. My last two jobs were in state institutions where I was forced to work through a maze of rules and bureaucrats. Regularly I watched the mentality of lawyers replace that of educators as tenure decisions and even stances in the classroom looked to what would hold up in court. This has conditioned, if not caused, a decline in personal responsibility that has gone hand in hand with a decline in care. People not trusted by the overseers of state monies have reduced their fiscal responsibility to spending as much as the auditors will allow. People not trusted to judge their colleagues intelligently and fairly have said, "To hell with it. Let the Dean decide." The institutions have been sending out unmistakable signals that credit-hour production will drive the whole process and that the financial bottom line will be the bodies herded into a classroom.

The state legislators have been so niggardly with pay raises that educators have lost considerable ground to inflation and higher education commands less and less respect. If you wanted to be highly prized in the community where my last school was located, you were better off owning a pizza parlor than teaching. Becoming an entrepreneur was the hottest game in town, business management was the expertise most prized, and fencing educators in with more and more regulations was the dominant trend. The worst of the legislative yahoos, who wanted to have professors punch time clocks and be in their offices from eight to five, have not won the day yet but the number of their supporters has clearly grown, and not all of them have come from outside the educational system. In upper echelons many efficiency experts (getting paid considerably more than senior professors) have been burning the midnight oil trying to plug the leaks in zero-based budgeting and make the educational system more efficient.

The farce of it all is that an educational system is maximally efficient only when all the parties involved, especially the teachers and students, are fired with a personal love of learning. The conditions of this love prominently include freedom and responsibility. When students can withdraw from courses with only a quarter of the course yet to run, students are not held responsible. When administrators allow this policy because it benefits the school financially (students are not being refunded money spent on dropped courses that do not count toward graduation), learning and probably also justice is being thwarted. The policies I would urge as consonant with the experience of learning, Christian ethics, and feminist wisdom, run exactly in the opposite direction. I would have fewer rules and more accountability. I would leave students considerably freer of required courses and test them considerably more rigorously.

In fiscal matters, my primary care would be to secure responsible people and create an atmosphere of trust. Then I would allocate monies to these people as income and budgetary priorities allowed, telling them to spend the monies as they determined would be best. Behind this would lie the conviction that a school would progress in the measure that it invited all the people party to its work into an energetic and fulfilling collaboration. Relatedly, I would want these people to experience their work as itself fulfilling. So I would take care that students not come to think of their courses as merely a means to a degree. And I would take care that younger faculty be rewarded for extra time spent on teaching and counseling. Presently students hear from the culture at large that education is mainly job training. Presently younger faculty hear from most large institutions that the only thing crucial is publishing. Both of these messages are careless almost to the point of criminality. The leadership that tolerates them (let alone the leadership that broadcasts them) has bankrupted its spiritual life. In schools where I have served the people grumbling most at this drift are humanists and feminists. The former know that business is not the first, or the fifth, or even the tenth most important of a university's concerns. The latter know that the going ways of running most schools, of conducting education, contradict the experiences and end-products they are supposed to be serving and taking care of.

· PERSUASION ·

There are women among the foolish administrators of depersonalized, careless institutions, certainly, and they are as culpable as their male counterparts. There are women whose first recourse is rules rather than persuasive argument and example, and I would call them as retarded as their male counterparts. But I find in feminine leadership, overall, an instructive resistance to depersonalization and legalism. I find a care and an instinctive reliance on persuasion that fit the Christian good news remarkably well.

For matters that significantly impinge on human welfare, any kind of compulsion, physical or legal, is a sorry tool. I know sometimes it seems the only effective tool because a given population is underdeveloped or even criminal. But whenever we speak of significant hopes and successes, we speak of things that require freedom and love. The family, for instance, cannot be what its critics or its own members want it to be unless both children and adults play their roles from conviction rather than compulsion. The church cannot be the community of Christ when its guiding force is canon law. A school is only an institution of learning when creativity and productivity rank higher than warm bodies and filled seats. A publishing firm whose first criterion of success is its financial statement is a menace we ought to leash. When the American Catholic bishops explore the economy of the United States and find that its guiding principles fail biblical standards, they remind all their readers that one cannot serve God and mammon. When feminists survey these forms of leadership, they confirm their conviction that effectiveness demands a full commitment to the ends and the means.

The Christian term for an experience through which we are moved to a personal affirmation of genuinely good ends and means is "conversion." People must be turned around, converted from the suasions of mammon. The persuasions of Christ, stemming from a deep union with a parental God and leading to such a union, would turn them with two strong hands. The first hand deals with the negative results being produced by un-Christian convictions. People who are edgy about a lack of fulfillment and meaning, and who are forced to admit that current systems are not doing the job or are even fomenting injustice, are fertile ground for the persuasions of the gospel. In this sense sin and disorder serve the gospel, for their ugliness and the suffering they produce bring many people to the conviction that there has to be a better way.

The second turning hand of Christ involves the more excellent way of charity, which Paul hymned in I Corinthians 13. When Jesus looked on the "people of the land" in his day, those suffering on the margins of that society, he relied on the love of his Abba to reveal how they might become blessed. When the disciples saw the glory of the transfigured Christ, they experienced the wholly positive dimension of the gospel, where the grace of God is seen to far exceed the healing of sin. Divinization, as the gratuitous fulfillment of our deepest human hopes for unlimited light and love, is the most powerful of the New Testament's persuasions. As brought home to us by the Holy Spirit, it removes any doubts that the more excellent way flows from God's own being.

The Spirit obviously does not compel people except in the paradoxical way of making unloving ways unattractive. The person wise by religious canons realizes more and more that unless she wins her interlocutor's heart she has at most won a tiny battle. Feminist instinct and Christian instinct converge at this heart of the political matter. People who want a polis prosperous by standards better than mammon's have to commit themselves to winning minds and hearts. The crux of the feminist intuition that one has to multiply colleagues, personally committed adherents, and friends is that liberty finally can be neither shortcircuited nor constrained. As God leaves people free, allowing them even to insult the divine grant of their being and life, so wise leaders leave people free, handing those they cannot persuade over to the ministrations of experience.

Our context for these reflections remains Christian orders, of course, and they harmonize with our prior arguments for women's candidacy. If women tend to persuade rather than to compel, and women's theoretical elaboration of their instincts about successful leadership runs to matters of the spirit or heart, then women appear amazingly close to the positions exemplified by the biblical Christ. On the whole, the biblical Christ served the cause of freedom, as Paul sang out in Galatians 5:1: "For freedom Christ has set us free." In the main, his message was the good news of the dawning of the Kingdom, not the bad news of the dawning of judgment. Furthermore, his appeal was pragmatic and experiential: consider the fruits a given tree is growing; look at the works God's messenger has performed. I cannot say that all feminist circles follow Christ completely in this orientation, but I can say that these foundations for Christian ministry strike me as a perfecting of feminist inclination.

How do we best avoid the violence and conflict that come when compulsions break down, if not by persuading people that peace and joy are better fruits? How do we free the gospel from charges of colonialism or vested self-interest if not by showing ourselves people willing to serve at cost? In families down the generations, many members have shown themselves willing to serve at cost, but certainly mothers have been prominent self-spenders. In the annals of church history many groups have asked little and given much, but certainly nuns have been prominent self-spenders. The special pathos of nuns recently has been their sense that all their sacrifices have been so little appreciated. Let them ask for control of their own lives, let alone an equal share with consecrated men in the church's leadership, and they feel the back of Rome's hand. The special pathos of mothers, not just recently but for centuries, has been the battering they risked for asking to control their own lives. To me this is persuasive evidence that non-feminist leadership in both domestic and church circles has proven inadequate. Indeed, it is persuasive evidence that this non-feminist leadership has proven abusive and pathological.

The more positive persuasion of feminist leadership, where it goes beyond avoiding the pathologies of leadership by compulsion or force, is its consonance with our better inclinations as the gospel reveals them. The good that we would do includes dealing with people in a kindly and patient way while sufficiently in possession of our souls and convinced of the rightness of our cause that we need lash out at no unbeliever. The evil that we would not do is to fall into a lack of conviction and consequent violence that we see displayed in different forms by Muslim fanatics, uncertain patriarchs, captains of industry, and rigid hierarchs of Catholic Christianity. The women who call their treatment by such hierarchs "nun-battering" may fall into rhetorical excess, but one should not miss their sense of hurt, nor fail to see how miserably church leadership has failed to persuade them. The unstrident, loving ministers who hold to the God of Jesus and try to make their rain fall and their sun shine on just and unjust alike recall to us better options. They try to persuade the way a mother tries to persuade a beloved child, or one tries to persuade a lover in danger of hurting himself. They try to persuade as the widow tried to persuade the unjust judge: not by throwing rocks through the windows of his chamber, but by wearing him down with the rightness of her cause.

· COURAGE ·

The courage hymned by the American media has all the profundity of the education applauded on the business page. Rocky and Rambo, the incredible hulks of our time, display a courage that stops at the level of superheated blood. This sells very well on the big screen so we see more and more of it. The boxer and the butcher steep us in images of gore, while battering and war keep going on.

In the antiseptic, air-conditioned laboratories where new nuclear weapons are designed courage has a more cerebral bent. Like chess masters forcing their minds to stricter strategies, our scientists and analysts rely on the genius of hyperlogic. Mutual assured destruction has become the regnant dogma there, and courage is facing the constant threat of nuclear war. Those who are real men stare at the scenarios of holocaust without blinking, so strong is their disdain of weaker values such as survival and common sense. It is all reminiscent of the dour existentialism of the 1950s, when the highest of human virtues was stoically enduring life's absurdity. Albert Camus made Sisyphus the representative figure. More recently Robert Heilbroner has proposed Atlas, the giant who bears the weight of the world. Neither author, it seems, gave a second thought to Christ, sensing that his comedic instinct finally mocks their pseudo-tragedy.

True courage, in Christian perspective, is following through on one's faith, hope, and love, despite all the opposition of Satan's minions. It is clinging to a Master who was despised, rejected, and hanged as a criminal because of the love and spiritual power that went out from him. To the unfaithful, the despairing, and the loveless it offers compassion rather than contempt. To those who would bemoan the impossibility of escaping the binds of mutual assured destruction, it offers the assurance that what was done by human folly may be undone by the human wisdom and repentance that grace can create. Jonathan Schell has followed up on his analytic work, *The Fate of the Earth*,[1] with a series of constructive proposals. In *The Abolition*[2] he takes the position that there is no conceivable situation in which unleashing nuclear weapons would do more good than harm. The consequence of this judgment (which finds support in the scientific community's warnings of a "nuclear winter") is a political stance significantly different from current policies of deterrence. Schell would have us do away with our stockpiles of nuclear weapons and rely only on our knowledge of how to make them, thus producing a considerably removed deterrent.

This is certainly progress over the current mentality, but it too fails the Christian standards of courage. For it too considers beyond the pale human beings' redemption or conversion into a rationality that could create world government, reworked economic relationships, and a new sense of what human intelligence ought to serve.

Yet these are the only solid programs on which to launch a safe future. That Christ suffered the cross because of human perversity is the Christian basis for doubting that human beings are wise or good enough not to destroy themselves. That Christ was willing so to suffer and that God raised Christ from the death that humanity, doing its worse, had inflicted upon him, are bases for the courage to act as though earth might one day be fair and all our children might one day see their grandchildren.

The women who have staked their lives outside the dim and brutal set of possibilities shown them by patriarchal cultures have acted in the lineaments of Christ's courage. Whether by praying to a God who seemed to be silent and wringing from him some practical help, or by stubbornly resisting moving to counter-hatred and destruction, many women have kept the wanton warriors from laying the whole earth to waste. Courage is not the capacity to muster blood and vengeance, impressive as that can sometimes be. Courage is the capacity to keep to the course of justice and love.

The Israel that kept faith with its covenanted Lord, or that at least repented of its transgressions, was more courageous than the Israel that dreamed of smashing the heads of enemy infants against rocks. For every Judith who beheaded the wicked enemy there were ten intimations of Lady Wisdom urging a deeper faith. The greatest of the writing prophets finally realized that none of the moves of the power-politicians was likely to win God's seconding. And so Jesus, the greatest of Christians' living prophets, modeled a way of spiritual resistance, convinced that the grace of his Father would always abound over sin. Each time that Christians summon the energy and courage to get back on this spiritual way, they confound the pundits of deterrence. Each time women listen to their nonviolent forebears, they keep the wisdom of God shining in a darkness always threatening to overwhelm it. The wisdom of God is wiser than men. The weakness of God is stronger than men. The laughter of God, for all its sad edge, is more real than the grimness of our warriors. Mother courage, as we might call it, has often taken this laughter to heart, mocking the deadly seriousness of the war-game players and keeping Christ as its general.

Today women who want to lead people to Christ have to muster the courage to face down the sexism of many Christian establishments. In spite of heavy conditioning, they often have to stand by their core instincts that many of the present ways of Catholic Christianity are simply wrong. A follower of Bernard Lonergan might call this the courage to accept the yield of one's best judgments, seeing the movement of the human spirit from experience through understanding to judgment as the God-given way we advance in the light. The love that raises this judgmental process to a higher plane does not remove the need to stand by the imperatives of judgment and decision. What the Spirit pours forth in our hearts may finally imply our granting the divine mystery a blank check, but there is no coda to the effect that we make this check out to our church's officials. Where Protestant Christianity speaks of the sovereignty of the Word of God over the church, Catholic Christianity must speak of the Holy Spirit and individual conscience. (In an ecumenical church, the insights of one group would be the insights of all, so one wouldn't have to keep searching for equivalents.) But with or without such supportive speech from their own Christian communities, feminists must find the courage to make clear distinctions between the essence of their faith and its many accidentals.

We shall return to these struggles of conscience when we reflect on the twists and turns of decisions about abortion. There one of our principal concerns will be that individual, autonomous decision-making not get so isolated from traditional wisdom and common sense that people cut themselves off from objective realities. Honesty and symmetry dictate that we make the same notation here, lest the judgmental and ethical courage that we are urging in ecclesiastical matters seem viciously subjective. No, my point is not to urge that women ignore the traditions from which the current laws of Catholic Christianity derive. It is simply to clear the way for women who find those traditions in conflict with current realities to experience their right to take their own lives in hand. Such women of course retain this right when it comes to hard decisions about abortion, divorce, or any other problem their lives may thrust upon them. There, as in this matter of orders and ecclesiastical sexism, each of us has to take responsibility for her stance. But in my opinion the great need in the question of orders and ecclesiastical sexism is for women to find the courage to turn the supposed traditions against themselves. Conversely, the great need I find in the matter of abortion is for Christian women to find the courage to turn away from the ideologues of both the right and the left and again confront the Spirit who would breathe in life.

· WISDOM ·

Throughout evolutionary history, the Spirit who would breathe in life has made all human beings, but especially women, willing to put themselves in peril, if that be the price for progeny and the race's continuance. What the American Indians called the killing-power of the warrior played an important role in this evolutionary process, but the more direct role obviously was played by the life-power of women. The Indians tabooed this life-power (and also the killing-power), not because it was dirty or polluting but because it conjured up the awesome ultimacy of the holy creative power by which all reality stood. When biblical peoples recorded their taboos on blood, they sometimes forgot this positive backdrop. Indeed, it was possible for them to virtually exempt men from taboos that would have prohibited service at the altar, when the warrior's way became passé and men did little bloodletting. (Bodily emissions remained a source of taboo, but these were usually operative only briefly.) The taboos on women's fertility-power tended to remain, however, and it seems clear they have played a powerful subconscious role in the historical decisions to keep women from the Christian altar. Today the part of wisdom, I believe, is to drag such underground prejudice out into the light, that we may see how little authority we should grant it.

Women's rather patient sense of wisdom has no doubt served the tribe well historically, especially when it came to precipitous decisions about war and destructiveness. In their own circles they have tended to talk things through, soliciting a sense of the faithful or consent of the whole body. As well, they have struck many traditional observers as better symbols of the natural Tao than men, because they have chosen persuasion and care to season their courage. Nowadays, however, the movement of women toward a full equality seems to be creating new sapiential models, or at least models with more nuance. In several impressive ones that I have seen, patience less connotes waiting for one's hopes to arrive than suffering for necessary changes through nonviolent action or resistance.

Prem Bodasingh, a young heroine in Alan Paton's moving novel *Ah, But Your Land Is Beautiful*,[3] might stand for this new version of feminist political wisdom. She fights against the apartheid law of South Africa by using the tactics of nonviolence now familiar from the campaigns of Mahatma Gandhi. Throughout her participation in the movement for change, she opposes the unjust status quo without herself becoming unjust or embittered. Even when she is defeated, in the sense of deprived of her sight by a retaliatory incident and forced to leave South Africa, she has triumphed, for she has contributed to the clarification of the apartheid mentality that now makes it synonymous with the darkness condemned by the author of John: "And this is the judgment, that the light has come into the world, and men loved darkness rather that light, because their deeds were evil" (John 4:19). If this is the crucial judgment in any political battle—which side better represents the divine light—women such as Prem make crucial contributions. In Deuteronomic terms, they dramatize the two ways, of life and of death, that God sets before us each day, putting themselves on the line or at risk for life. So doing, they continue women's millennial devotion to life-power.

Feminist leadership, as I envision it, puts itself on the line for life. It uses its own roots in subjugation and marginality to dramatize the most important issue in any controversy. It does not do this simplistically, of course, nor without confessing how the complexity of many political situations humbles it. But it keeps faith with an almost uterine instinct that wisdom is the way of life, and that foolishness is the way that says there is no God and so makes death the great inevitability. A Helen Caldicott, speaking as a physician and mother, cuts to the heart of the controversies about nuclear power and arms-building, because she keeps front and center the value of life. Until we gain the capacity to transmute radioactive materials, our nuclear power plants will keep increasing the mortgage we hold on the life of nature's ecosystems. Until we regain control of human war making, nuclear energy will haunt us like the angel of death. Wisdom simplifies many of the political balance sheets by pressing this bottom line. If a given proposal is more likely to endanger life than to secure or enhance it, that proposal is prima facie stupid.

Gloria Steinem, another impressive leader, displays a similar gravitation toward life. Again and again the drift of her analysis or argument is toward what will better defend us against death and injustice, what will better enhance the quality of human life. One may quarrel with certain of Steinem's interpretations of this basic criterion, as I shall concerning abortion, but her overall program seems to me remarkably wise. Indeed, religious people like me regularly need a recall like hers to the importance of this-worldly living. If our God cannot improve things for battered women, for victims of racial discrimination and others leading hopeless lives, how can we speak of our God as a God of life? If the gospel we preach does not bring joy and fulfillment, how can our leadership be persuasive? When I watch Steinem rely on charity, competence, reason, and above all wit, I see many of the traditions of feminist wisdom updated. The keen eye of the outsider combines with the sometimes acerbic debunking of the prophetess to superbly satiric effect. Machismo, it becomes even clearer, is a stupid and lumbering brute. Lady Wisdom, rolling her eyes and shaking her head, wonders how long, O Lord, how long?

Women have had the wisdom to lead revolutions or revolts in taste and sensibility by such satiric methods. They have tended to rely on their intuitions of life's holism and sanctity to debunk the savageries of war and oppression. The more reflective of them have seen the place for drive and aggression. The more religious have wondered about the crooked lines with which providence writes without ceasing to praise the divine mystery. Feminist wisdom today cannot abandon this deeper sort of reflection. When Thomas Aquinas observed that the property of the wise person is to give order, he assumed that the framework is always religious or ultimate. Women's work of mothering, teaching, nursing, and praying has given them as much access to this ultimate framework as men. Even when theology or higher education seemed to limit such access, the experience of daily life reopened the doors. The feminine persona of both the biblical Sophia and the Buddhist Prajnaparamita suggest that the order wise people have found, West and East, has been subtle and full of grace. This has no end of lessons for those who would help us choose life today, including those who pontificate about competence for orders.

Lady Wisdom is subtle and indirect, because gross and assaultive ways so regularly miss the mark. Lady Wisdom is full of grace because truth finally is beautiful, as well as completely dependent on God. For the wise, a wink is as good as a nod. One need not belabor a point or elaborate one's laws. For the wise, harmony and clarity are crucial indices of truth. Thus Doris Lessing, describing a city of health and wisdom, takes pains to show its roundness and pleasing colors.[4] Reality, Lady Prajnaparamita would say, moves along like a stream or a dance. To stay in touch with it, or be connected, one must oneself move gracefully. Salvation, Lady Sophia would say, is a gift manifestly beyond us. Unless the Lord goes before and supports throughout, we remain sources of hurtful disorder. Beyond salvation, in the realm of divinization, the truth is if anything still more gracious. The divine life the Lady hymns is so fully a pulsation of love that God must pluck out our old hearts of stone and give us new hearts of flesh. As the Lady Wisdom played these tunes before God, encoding them in the music of the spheres, so must she play them today. Our feminist leadership will never be fully wise until it centers in graciousness.

·5·

WOMEN'S PRIESTHOOD

· LIKENESS TO CHRIST ·

The leadership women have exerted historically and continue to exert today fits them for the official Christian ministries. Like women's work, both historical and contemporary, it suggests that a church wanting to tap the best and the brightest for its priesthood is foolish in the extreme to disdain the female half of the race. Studies such as Lawrencé Cunningham's two interesting volumes, *The Meaning of Saints* and *The Catholic Heritage*, support this generalist argument that I have been building.[1] The women we meet in such books are as holy and wise as the men. Whether the topic is sainthood or tradition, sex is nothing determinative. So, unless the priesthood bears no connections to sainthood and tradition, sex should not be determinative of one's fitness for orders.

This argument from common sense and common historical experience is redoubled when one considers the priesthood now either being practiced by female Protestant ministers or sought by female Catholics. The argument of the Roman Curia that women lack the likeness to Christ essential for representing Christ ministerially breaks apart as soon as one is willing to look at what actually is occurring. Thus theologians across a wide span of Christianity, from Karl Rahner to Elisabeth Schüssler-Fiorenza, poke holes in the curial argument.[2] On the one hand, they dispute the assumption that the likeness to Christ essential for an orthodox or effective Christian ministry is physical or genital. On the other hand, they note that women played roles in the early church whose equivalents today would imply priesthood or even episcopacy, and that the crux of all Christian priesthood is the capacity for the sort of service and mediation that is discussed in Hebrews, the writing of the New Testament that meditates most fully on priesthood.

The burden of Hebrews is to argue typologically that Jesus has fulfilled the priesthood, sacrifice, and covenant of his Israelite people. In making this argument, the author stresses the humanity of Christ and his passibility. Because of his full identification with us in vulnerable flesh, he can sympathize with our weaknesses: "Since then we have a great high priest who has passed through the heavens, Jesus, the Son of God, let us hold fast our confession. For we have not a high priest who is unable to sympathize with our weaknesses, but one who in every respect has been tempted as we are, yet without sin. Let us then with confidence draw near to the throne of grace, that we may receive mercy and find grace to help in time of need" (4:14–16).

If today we should ask our priestly servants to give us an updated version of this basis for holding fast to our confession of faith and feeling that our representative before God fully sympathizes with our human condition, how would we likely find ourselves thinking? The one whom our priest follows, Jesus, has passed through the heavens; he is one who belongs to God and has the divine sphere as his home. Consequently, we should expect our priests to be people of spiritual conviction and depth who know well the difference between God and mammon and have staked their lives on God. If we find ourselves criticizing our priests as too little distinguished from worldlings, too little formed by the divine transcendence, we shall be saying, at least implicitly, that they are not matching the template of Christ the high priest, whose Father always remained his first treasure. On the other hand, if we find ourselves criticizing our priests as too aloof from their people, insufficiently aware of human weaknesses or sympathetic toward them, we shall be saying that the solidarity with his people that Christ showed no longer appears in our priests' profile. In such a case the rational move would probably be to rethink the requirements for our priesthood and try to remove what seems to be dehumanizing its membership. We might discover, to few people's surprise, that celibacy and aversion from women stand high among the likely culprits. Then we would only need the courage to follow through on our discovery and change our requirements. The parallel in the case of the transcendent di-

mension of the Christian priesthood probably would lead us to re-
structure ministerial formation so as to focus more starkly on spirituality and political witness. If we, the Christian people as a whole,
found those who ought to be carrying on Christ's high priesthood
among us insufficiently resident in "heaven," the most promising
antidote would surely be increasing our demand that priests learn
the lessons of both petitionary prayer and the prophets' clamor for
justice.

It will not have escaped the attentive reader, of course, that this
reflection assumes the relevance of the Christian people's impressions of how well their priests are following Christ. The "likeness"
that ought to be in question finally roots in the hypostatic union
central to the mystery of the Incarnation. Unless those who symbolize the mediatorship of Jesus Christ actually re-present his connection of heaven above and earth below, making God's gracious
divinization of humanity credible in this our time, they fail their
first reason to be. Indeed, an astute theology of Christian ministry
would examine candidates principally on the issue of their potential
for extending Christian incarnationalism. Especially in Catholic
Christianity, the sacramentalism through which Johannine Christology or incarnationalism of any orthodox stripe extends itself is
always a matter of graciously anointing human flesh—cleansing
what has been dirtied, feeding what has become ravenous for want
of bread and wine. To cut through to the heart of the feminist position: Who seriously can argue that women are less apt for this sort
of priesthood than men?

Hebrews goes on to enrich its central concern for a mediator well
situated between heaven and weak humanity, stressing the sufferings of Christ our high priest. On the cross he became not only the
mediator who presides over the sacrifice (the complete handing
over of humanity to God) but the victim who bore all of humanity's
ugliness and sin. This was no easy task, and the obedience that Jesus
showed to the divine plan that required it was only learned at a
high cost. In another passage to which an astute theology of priesthood would frequently return, the author puts it quite starkly: "In
the days of his flesh, Jesus offered up prayers and supplications,
with loud cries and tears, to him who was able to save him from
death, and he was heard for his godly fear. Although he was a Son,
he learned obedience through what he suffered; and being made

perfect he became the source of eternal salvation to all who obey him, being designated by God a high priest after the order of Melchizedek" (5:7–10).

Let me attempt a contemporary paraphrase: Fully human, Jesus was driven by the trials of life to cry out to God honestly, boldly, from the depths of his spirit. He trusted that God, however apparently silent and careless, would be offended by his battering and so would come to his aid. This attitude of trust pleased the Father, who always kept Jesus as the apple of his eye, and the Father was moved to resurrect Jesus from the worst that human disorder was able to inflict upon him. The sufferings that Jesus underwent taught him in his bones that God is the only one worth serving, because God is the only one to whom history finally must bow. This wisdom, we might say, makes Jesus the source of healing and divinization for all human beings who interpret their sufferings in his terms. If they cry out to God, when they have done all that they themselves can do and they still find themselves being battered or discriminated against, the solutions they receive will come from the heaven that Jesus opened when he split the Temple veil.

If such a paraphrase is at all acceptable, we see how like Jesus the sacrificial victim many women historically have been. As well, we see how easy it would be to place women at the Christian altar, if church leaders only knew their Scriptures.

· LEARNING ·

The learning put forward by Hebrews as crucial to Christ's priesthood certainly is nothing bookish or guaranteed by a seminary curriculum. The obedience in which priestly learning ought to issue mainly comes from the pains of daily religious living. So the prime population from which one would expect the Christian priesthood to come is the same population addressed by the beatitudes. Those who learn that blessedness seldom is the benefaction of the rich and powerful; those who have hungered and thirsted for a justice seldom available in time; those who are meek and dedicated to peacemaking—they are the ones learned in the ways of the Kingdom.

Liberation theology has taken this central thrust of Jesus' preaching to heart, reasoning that the best church will be that which comes closest to the poor, the marginal, the people on the broad lower tier of society. So the ecclesiology of the liberation theologians stresses "basic communities," in which the people as a whole minister the good news to one another. Belatedly, because of Latin American machismo, liberation ecclesiology has also begun to champion the rights of women. At Puebla, the most recent meeting of the Conference of Latin American bishops and their theologians, this championship had not yet progressed to the point of challenging the church's denial of ordination to women, but such a challenge would seem simply a matter of time, as long as the liberation theologians keep faith with their preferential option for the poor.

What have we begun to learn about the priesthood by consulting the experiences of grass-roots churches and those who minister to the poor? First, that an effective priesthood demands close identification with one's people, as evident in a book compiled by the Nicaraguan priest Ernesto Cardenal. Ministering to the little community of Solentiname, he not only solicited the reactions to the gospel from all the people attending the liturgy, he also plainly shared the concerns and needs of all these people. The oppressive dictatorship of Anastasio Somoza and his henchmen ground Cardenal down as much as it did his *campesinos*. The priest in the center of such a liturgical circle suffered from the sexism hurting the women as much as any man could.

Second, we have learned that priestly learning comes in good measure from listening to one's people. Tradition helps, of course, but if those who are ordained are going to continue to grow in wisdom and grace before God and the human community, they have to hear what the Holy Spirit is saying to the seven churches (Rev. 1:4), to sense what new ecclesiastical forms the trials and joys of the common people are conceiving. A model of the church in which the priest's first allegiance is to an institutional chain of command is vicious for at least two reasons. It in fact divorces the common people who have been baptized from its operative images of "the church," and it ignores the constituency that all ecclesiastical command ought to be serving. Orders in the church exist for the whole church's flourishing. Whenever orders of any kind—priesthood, episcopacy, or papacy—become a preserve on their own, neither the vine nor the branches is being well served.

One can understand the tendency of even generous ministers to start to think of the church as belonging more to them than to the whole people of God. However, this is not the sort of understanding that translates into forgiveness. The name we rightly give such arrogation of ecclesiastical ownership by those in orders is "clericalism," and it is not a term of either praise or endearment. Clericalism is the priest's version of the Augustinian brand of sin: love of self unto contempt for God and God's purposes. When clericalism occurs in patterns that clearly follow the lines of gender, as it does in Catholic Christianity, one has sinful self-centeredness compounded by sinful sexism. Then the leadership of a church has so much to learn that one must start praying for its conversion. Huge portions of the community at large find the priesthood incredible, as is now the Catholic case. I can think of no more dramatic way of expressing conversion back to the egalitarian standards of Christ than for the present leadership to put away its deafness and stony disapproval and begin really listening to what the seven sisters are saying.

Among the clearest sermons being preached by the women now actually serving as ordained Christian ministers is the integral connection between sexism and social disorder as a whole. Thus Lora Gross, co-pastor of the Augustana Lutheran church in Omaha, Nebraska, has put the connection in terms of basic incarnationalism or embodiment: "Every day as we begin our work, we are confronted by the harsh realities of urban life—poverty, racism, crime. All tear deeply at the social fabric and challenge the church's rhetoric of love, justice, and wholeness. As we've sought to define our ministry in Omaha, I've found myself drawn to a query by James Nelson whether there is an interconnection between human sexuality and the broken relationship among human beings that is at the very roots of social injustice. . . . Establishing the connection between issues of human sexuality and justice challenges the church's theology of social ministry in three ways. First, it challenges it to embrace a body-self presence in and to the world. Second, it challenges it to confront and transform abuses of patriarchal power, which is the undergirding of social injustice. Third, it challenges it to define, develop, and integrate an androgynous experience of empowerment for individuals and social institutions, including the church."[3]

A ministry in touch with the realities of our torn social life therefore finds sexism part and parcel of the regime that the Kingdom of Christ would oust. As well, it finds androgyny—the full male-femaleness of the human species—prominent among the qualities that the Kingdom would establish in our time. A ministerial corps that admits female candidates as the equals of males is a giant step toward the androgyny that the Kingdom should offer as the counter to today's sexism. A ministerial corps in which married couples can function as teams is even further progress, since it makes the androgyny in question as complementary as Christian marriage and parenthood can demand. When Catholic Christianity becomes humble and ecumenical enough to admit the data of Protestant ministers as directive for its own priestly reforms, it will find a broader experience of mediation with a richer representation of the full range of Christ's likeness to us in all things save sin.

· ADMINISTRATION ·

Of the studies of Catholic Christian ministry that have appeared in recent years, the well-rounded expertise of the team that produced *Parish, Priest and People* at first blush recommends it highly.[4] For feminist readers, however, the book proves quite disappointing. Neither the sociologists nor the theologians show much sign of anticipating a Catholic priesthood for women. Indeed, their closing recommendations ignore the issue of women's ordination completely. One doesn't know whether the authors are simply insensitive to the hopes of numerous Catholic women and the androgynous needs of the Catholic people at large or whether they have chosen to ignore the question of women's ordination as presently imprudent to ponder. Either way, they strike me as failing to read the signs of the times and as disturbingly mired in the status quo. If they are the green wood, no wonder the priesthood of Catholic Christianity is liable to so much criticism.

This study does have the merit of drawing close to the actual exercise of Christian ministry in Catholic parishes, however, and therefore of bringing out the administrative dimensions of the priest's work. Of course, one can argue that administration has little to do with the core of Christian orders, and that most administrative tasks in the church can be done by laypeople as fittingly as by priests. Perhaps for this reason most studies of the possibility of ordaining women to the Catholic Christian priesthood pay administrative tasks little heed. Nonetheless, here and there one finds snippets of current public perception or past Christian precedent, and setting them in the context of our generalist reflection on women's aptness for orders may prove stimulating.

Emily C. Hewett and Suzanne R. Hiatt, writing about priesthood for women in the Episcopal church, note that one of the popular objections to the idea of women priests was that people would not be able to imagine how such priests would actually function. This seems more a judgment on church people that an argument against women's ordination, but it may be that such a viewpoint was quite influential. The authors' own analysis, written in 1973, before the ordination of women was adopted by the Episcopal Church, began with the matter of administration, but quickly shifted to the image conjured up when Episcopalians had to contemplate women leading the Sunday liturgy: "Though the objection to women rectors is often initially supported by the contention that women do not make good administrators or that they lack the authority to hold a parish together, illustrations of women administrators in other fields fail to lay it to rest. The reason is that the real objection is aesthetic—we simply cannot imagine Sunday services being led by a woman. We feel that the liturgy demands a bass, or at least a baritone voice to do it justice. Women's voices do not ring with the authority and power we find so comforting in the familiar liturgy."[5] One would like to think that so simple an expedient as taking the unimaginative lay leaders of a balky congregation down the street to a church in which a woman was presiding and preaching effectively would have answered this objection, but visceral instinct insists that minds made up are not likely to be confused by evidence to the contrary.

The history of Catholic Christianity, to be sure, furnishes us few examples of women exercising priestly administration, unless one is willing to translate "priestly" with a bit of latitude. Then the jurisdiction exercised by women religious leaders, such as medieval abbesses, or the brisk competence shining through the religious leadership of a Teresa of Avila, quickly makes the case that female priests ought a priori to be judged neither less nor more capable of good administration. In the matter of medieval precedent, a paragraph from Haye van der Meer's *Women Priests in the Catholic Church?* ought to suffice:

the entire exterior and interior direction and administration of the congregation under her. She had to bestow all prebends, churches, benefices, offices, and canonicates in her church. From the bull of Nicholas V (in the middle of the fifteenth century) to the foundation of Gandersheim it follows that the abbess had an "ordinary authority" in addition. In the fifteenth century the abbess of Vreeden had to warn, suspend, or dismiss and discharge completely the male members of the foundation whenever they were negligent.[6]

More in keeping with our overall exposition than these windows onto current sociology and past history, however, is a feminist reflection on religious administration itself. Is there anything sexually determined about the skills that go into good administration in religious matters? Are women intrinsically unqualified to deal with either the foundational, or the middling, or the niggling concerns that any administrator must face? I've never seen a study that suggested a positive answer to this question, and certainly my observations of male and female administrators in higher education, including my observations at two schools where I have served as department head, turn up nothing to prompt one. In my impression, women presently are probably a little more apt than men to handle well the bigger issues of admitting the divine mystery and orienting decisions toward the upbuilding of life. They are also probably more apt to handle well the myriad small details that any significant project soon comes to include. They may well be more apt to tolerate institutional evils longer than is ideal, because of a greater aversion to conflict. But these considerations could easily turn up counter-indications—data suggesting that women are more sensitive to institutional injustice or that men better handle certain kinds of details. What nowhere seems indicated is a biological or sociological argument that women cannot organize tasks, supervise staffs, or direct an ongoing flow of communication as well as their male counterparts. From the secretary who is the real organizer of the executive's touted efficiency to the mothers who run the thousands of local organizations on which national life depends, women right now are administering—literally, showing marvelous "service-to" (the etymology of the word)—great portions of American life. In religiously based institutions, such as many Catholic schools and hospitals, nuns and laywomen alike are showing themselves as crisp, or as objectionable, as men. I think that women's personalism especially suits them for the administration of religious groups, in which the pains and joys of individuals ought always to be high on the agenda, but even this may be my dangerous stereotype.

Last, let me remind the reader that the early Catholicism developing in such documents as the Pastoral Epistles of the New Testament took a patriarchal slant from the surrounding Graeco-Roman culture and Jewish traditions. This determined that the leading administrators in the church would be male bishops or presbyters. The egalitarianism of the Jesus movement offered the foundations for a Christian ministry free of sexual bias, but when the church decided that gaining the good opinion of the surrounding culture was a matter of first priority, the possibility of an official female Christian leadership was bound to lessen. Throughout subsequent Christian history women have of course run a great many church affairs but not, in later Catholicism, as official priests.

· MEDIATION ·

Perhaps the key symbol in traditional Catholic reflection on ministerial orders or priesthood has been that of mediation. Catholic theology has not denied the more prophetic orientation toward service that has predominated in Protestant reflection on ministry, but it has made more of the bridge-building ("pontification") suggested by the sacrificial views of Hebrews. Strangely enough, however, the mentality that has insisted on likeness to Christ has not insisted on full likeness to the humanity being represented before God, as my sense of logic says that it should. Jesus certainly could represent humanity before God, and prior to separatist feminist sentiments few people argued that his maleness kept Jesus from functioning as the savior and high priest of women as well as men. In other words, the masculine sex of Jesus has not been deemed an impediment to his representation of women. Why, then, should the feminine sex of women who would serve as priests not be able to represent Jesus, or any other men whom their ministerial mediation would serve? Why, in fact, hasn't the rather obvious fact that an androgynous, male-female priesthood better represents humanity as a whole than a priesthood limited to either sex not led those concerned for symbolic symmetry to hasten to round out the ranks of the church's mediators?

In addition to this argument from the human side of the mediational flow that courses between heaven and earth, there is an argument from the heavenly side. It is not an argument that has wielded great influence to date, but it is gathering steam year by year. This is the logic of representing an androgynous or transsexual God by the full repertoire of human characteristics. Rosemary Ruether and others have written of the God-ess or feminine aspects of the transcendent divinity.[7] William Thompson has recently taken this divine femininity into the heart of Christology.[8] To my mind it is again simply common sense to fill out the theology of priestly mediation with a feminine representation to better render all the mothering, nurturing, creative, caring, and playful aspects of divinity that religions, biblical and Eastern alike, have associated with a bisexual ultimate reality.

Apart from the strictly theological issues involved in this potential recasting of the Catholic Christian understanding of orders, and admitting that the whole idea of "representing" the divinity has serious liabilities or dangers, let me now concentrate on the de facto mediation and representation that women are accomplishing. For it is clear to all those with eyes to see that mothers loving their children to health, teachers showing students something of ultimate wisdom, nurses showing the sick a tender care, counselors rebuilding fellowship and reconciling enemies, and simple friends giving one another attention, interest, and concern all mediate divine grace and represent well the parental God announced by Jesus. All, in fact, call to mind the priestly character and great dignity of the whole people of God, as I Peter gave it classical expression: "But you are a chosen race, a royal priesthood, a holy nation, God's own people, that you may declare the wonderful deeds of him who called you out of darkness into his marvelous light" (2:9). This text has buttressed the Protestant stress on the priesthood of all the faithful, and it should guide our interpretation of the widespread mediation of grace that so-called laypeople accomplish every day. Certainly women are as prominent as men in these ordinary instances of mediation, so certainly it is legitimate to speak of women already functioning in priestly fashion in Catholic Christianity. If the ordinary should weigh more heavily than the extraordinary, the priesthood of Catholic women should present few experiential problems.

To bolster this line of thinking, scholars occasionally note that the biblical tradition obviously admitted the prophecy of women, and that the distinctions between prophecy and priesthood are far from hard and fast. Thus Paul K. Jewett, dealing with several strands of biblical tradition, sees the legitimacy of women's prophetic office as calling in question any veto on women's ordination:

> The prophet is one who speaks for God to the people (cf. Heb. 1:11); the priest is one who speaks for the people to God (cf. Heb. 5:1). The reason that this difference is sometimes mentioned with regard to women and the ministry is not far to seek. The priesthood of the Old Testament was strictly limited to males, as was the apostolate in the New. In the Old Testament, however, some women were endowed with the gift of prophecy (II Kings 22:14); and at Pentecost the Spirit is said to have come not only upon sons but upon daughters as well (Acts 2:17–18), some of whom prophesied even in the assembled congregation (I Cor. 11:15). This being so, it becomes necessary, if one believes women are not to receive ordination, to explain why the function of a prophet is compatible, while that of a priest is incompatible, with a woman's place in the church.... In any case, whenever one tries to state it precisely, this argument that priests differ from prophets comes to grief so far as it is used to bar women from ordination.[9]

Actually, all the arguments used to bar women from ordination come to grief, except the argument from the predominant past practice and viewpoint of Catholic Christianity. Only if people believe that a male priesthood is essential to preserving the unchangeable portion of tradition can they continue to forbid orders to competent women. But this, too, is an argument hard to make, unless one has a rather positivistic or fundamentalist reading of tradition. A critical reading, on the contrary, takes the past seriously but also stays open to what the Spirit may be urging in the present. If the Spirit seems to be urging a development or deeper appreciation of essential parts of the tradition that cast accidental or more peripheral parts in a new light, then innovation is neither heretical nor imprudent. In fact, innovation can be fidelity to the deeper instincts of authentic tradition and a proper removal of interpretations of what should be handed on that were crippled by bias or provincialism.

This was the sort of argument both assumed and partially explicated by many of the participants in the Conference on Women and the Catholic Priesthood that drew 2,000 people to Detroit in November of 1975. As a statement drafted by Rosalie Muschal-Reinhardt put it:

> We have been called to the priesthood, and we want to be ordained, not because we want to exercise power, but because we are motivated by love and a concern for our Church. Indeed, we are already functioning as ministers, but under limitations and handicaps, owing to the lack of official recognition and authorization for our ministry, especially in the sacramental area. A major focus of the love and concern that move us is our firm conviction that we as women are indispensable to the full humanness and wholeness of the priesthood. Unquestionably, new models of priesthood are needed. We believe that women in the priesthood will inevitably produce those sorely needed new models. We call on the people of God to engage in dialogue on the nature of ministry and priesthood. We applaud and affirm the model of priesthood as presented in Hebrews 7:12, for when there is a change in the priesthood there is necessarily a change in the law as well.[10]

Hebrews 7:12, which the last line of the quotation virtually reproduces, implies a hermeneutics or theory of interpretation more like the critical one we sketched above than either a fundamentalist or a positivist sense of tradition. Tradition is alive, and ultimately only those who have the Spirit of God can read what it is signing for present times. The pity of this statement from the Detroit Conference is that it is now ten years old and Catholic women seem no closer to achieving the official priesthood. No wonder so many have given up on the Catholic hierarchy and either put their faith to work outside the church or felt that faith itself atrophy.

* Part II *

ABORTION

ABORTION

My proposal has been that by considering ordination and abortion we might gain a firm and useful purchase on Catholic feminist spirituality. We have now finished our consideration of ordination and are about to begin our consideration of abortion, so perhaps it is time for a pause or creative interlude.

Ordination for women became a live issue in Catholic Christianity in the early 1970s. The Detroit Conference held in November of 1975 cast a bright spotlight on the issue for American women, but in both the United States and Europe prior rumblings could have been heard for at least five years. On October 15, 1976, the Vatican, then under the direction of Pope Paul VI, issued its famous declaration to the effect that women would not soon be considered fit candidates for the Roman Catholic priesthood. That declaration certainly did not change the mind of many women convinced that the time was ripe for women's ordination, but it did dampen the hopes of those longing for institutional change. In fact, when combined with Paul VI's encyclical on birth control of 1968, the Vatican declaration convinced feminists that Roman Catholicism was one of its most powerful contemporary foes. The positive things that Pope Paul VI, and his successors John Paul I and John Paul II, have said about women, motherhood, social justice, and the rest have not removed this strongly negative judgment that feminists have formed. With more than a little justice, feminists look on such positive statements as palliatives—easy bits of praise cast like crumbs by those who will fight to the death for their patriarchal privileges. (The figure is not purely hyperbolic, since the lack of priests in many areas is seriously threatening the vitality of Catholic Christianity.)

Reflecting on all of this, I have been led to the judgment that the institutional sexism of Roman Catholicism, as its ban on women's ordination epitomizes, forces those who would develop a contemporary feminist spirituality from this tradition to move to deeper, indeed radical, ground. They must listen to the arguments of their magisterial leaders, be certain that in conscience they in fact cannot accept them, and then take responsibility for distinguishing their allegiance to Christ and the core of the Catholic Christian tradition from their allegiance to popes and curial officials. For those who suffered from the controversies over birth control that afflicted Roman Catholicism in the 1960s, this will seem quite familiar ground. But the rise of feminist sentiments and convictions in the 1970s has exacerbated things for many Catholic women. Those whom I consider wisest have passed through the fires and can speak of many aspects of their church's sexism humorously. But many others, who may by other standards be no less wise, have found their religious allegiance moving in other directions. They certainly have not been lost to God, but they have been lost to Catholic Christianity, and there is little reason to expect their speedy return.

My own experience and position, which may be more relevant in a general, reflective work such as this than in a scholarly one, has been more humorous than dolorous. I have never felt called to the Catholic priesthood, and I have always taken the pretensions of the Catholic hierarchy with many grains of salt. This is not to say that I have not felt discrimination in the Catholic church nor seen the ugly face of its sexism. As a nun for fifteen years I learned very well that the church is a several tiered society, and that priests rank far higher than religious women. One had only to look at the large parish rectory housing two or three priests in quite comfortable suites and compare it with the smaller construction housing eight to ten nuns to know the real rules of the game. That a teaching order such as mine had to wait until well into the 1960s to secure a policy of giving all its members a chance for a college education before rushing them out to staff parochial schools was another unmistakable signal. Pastors wanted larger bodies to care for all the little bodies they were herding into their parish schools. The preparedness of those larger bodies was a secondary consideration (and the personal fulfillment of the nuns themselves was beyond the pale).

When I chose to leave the convent, married, and secured a job teaching in a minor seminary in the Archdiocese of San Francisco, I found sexism continuing to dog me. One day the president of the seminary called me in to tell me that the archbishop had discovered my status (ex-nun married to ex-priest) and told him to fire me—on whatever grounds he thought best. Fortunately (since my pittance was the only salary we had) the president was more Christian than the archbishop so my firing never eventuated. But I realized beyond a doubt that uppity women could easily find themselves bugs in the path of the chancery steamroller.

A considerable part of the pathos I find in Catholicism's role in the recent American controversies over abortion stems from this radical realization. Women no doubt vary considerably in their experiences of abortion, but my guess is that there are relatively few women who do not find it traumatic. It is not difficult to imagine that many women are in fact brought into crisis by either the prospect or the actual occurrence of abortion and so are especially in need of the good news of Christ's grace. One can interpret Catholic teachings and practices about abortion as attempts to succor such women, but that takes a fund of good will that feminists—in fact any people committed to the proposition that women are as human as men—will find hard to muster. The record of Catholic Christianity with regard to women is abysmal. The refusal to admit women's competence for ordination is, to my mind, the most revealing of official Catholicism's positions, showing the church to be seriously warped by what a Marxist, or any person of stout common sense, would call ideological self-interest. Consequently, I can excuse feminists' deafness to the Catholic views of abortion. Until my church makes itself a credible advocate of women's full equality and prosperity, I too will practice a hermeneutic of suspicion regarding all its official statements.

This said, I must allow that I find the core of the Catholic Christian position on abortion not only ringing true but also casting a brilliant, much-needed light of common sense on a terribly confused battle ground. Common sense—not so much in Lonergan's potentially pejorative use of the term as in the tradition of the Scottish realists—is the perspective and instinct we can employ when our spirits are rightly ordered by the mystery of God and the complexity of human behavior. It is the remarkable trait, attributed to Dr. Johnson, of being able to see and honor the obvious. I find it obvious that widespread abortion manifests cultural sickness. When a people terminates fetal life easily, even casually, its culture is badly twisted.

Soon after the first imperative of ethics—do good and avoid evil —the human spirit receives the call to nurture life and avoid death. We invoke this call when we recoil in horror at the buildup of nuclear arms, or at the Nazi attempts at genocide, or at ecological devastation. We cloak ourselves in its mantle when we fight for the poor, whose spiritual if not physical lives are under assault, and when we struggle for women's liberation. But too many people in our society stop their ears and close their minds when the call is to protect the life begun in women's wombs. That seems to me at one and the same time profoundly unethical, un-Christian, and anti-feminist. It is an abomination from the outset and at the end, no matter how many qualifications and distinctions one must make in the political middle. True, not having had an abortion (although once having been forced to deal with the possibility of an unwanted birth), I should temper this rhetoric with due humility. As well, I want to temper it with sisterly compassion. In all honesty, however, I must warn the reader that I find abortion repulsive. Consequently, I find efforts to make easy abortion a standard part of the feminist platform repulsive and burdensome. As the sexism of Catholic Christianity has in my imagination taken on the lineaments of the cross, so the obtuseness or twisted secularism of dogmatic abortionism has become cruciform, threatening to make my second allegiance as bent and torn as my first. This double cross certainly afflicts many women more existentially than it afflicts me, but even in my case it has summoned the transcendence of God. With both of the movements that I would want to honor and serve showing themselves so imperfect and sinful, the sole adequacy of the divine silence and the cross of Christ has become more obvious. The Catholic feminist spirituality I see them creating will no more put its trust in secularist sisters than in sexist princes of the church.

·6·

CHRISTIAN THEORY

· CREATION ·

The first conviction that separates followers of the biblical God from secularists is enshrined in the Christian doctrine of creation. "In the beginning God created the heavens and the earth," the first line (Genesis 1:1) of the Bible runs, and no later theological sophistication ever surpasses the conviction that all that exists stems from a fontal divine source. Nearly equally important is the refrain (Genesis 1:4, 1:10, 1:12, 1:18, 1:21, 1:25, 1:31), "And God saw that it was good," which believers ought to make basic for all their evaluations of creation. As come from God (and going back to God), whatever exists has ontological value. Relatedly, nothing that exists is something that we, as mere creatures, can abuse at our whim or pleasure. We did not create it, even when we may have molded it or developed it marvelously, so we do not have the right to destroy it casually. Whatever destruction we feel forced to cause or abet must be justified by higher necessities and motives.

Many people of religious or simply ecological sensibility concur in this reverential attitude toward creation. Confronting a marvel of nature such as "El Capitan," the breathtaking rock face of Yosemite Valley, they instinctively feel it should be appreciated, applauded, and enjoyed, not defaced or assaulted. Gazing out over coastal waters or even desert wastes, they know that humanity is not the measure of significance. Much as the religiously devout person feels the arching space of a great cathedral as a welcome invitation to bow low and pray, so the person of natural sensitivity feels the vast spread of physical creation as a pressure to acknowledge the smallness of human beings, to express a proper humility. All the more so is this the case when the nature in question is the galactic universe, vaster than our imaginations can appreciate, or the sub-atomic world that reads us nearly incomprehensible lessons in the explosive force of primal matter.

The Christian doctrine of creation is therefore nothing esoteric. It deals with matters of common human experience, even though it sets those matters in a distinctive framework. For the Israelites whose experiences and insights fashioned the matrix of the Hebrew Bible, the significance of nature could not be divorced from the significance of what they considered a redemptive history. The God of the Exodus, who had liberated them from slavery in Egypt and set them in a promised land flowing with milk and honey, was the same divinity they intuited controlled the foundations of all creation. Genesis, many of the Psalms, Job, and portions of the pro-phetic literature all testify that creation and redemption or libera-tion were complementary panels in an Israelite dyptich. Because of the steadfast love Israel found at the core of its mysterious divinity (who was just what time or his revelatory good pleasure showed him to be; see Exodus 3:14), the natural world in which it lived and moved and had its being had to be confessed as in principle very good. Indeed, insofar as human beings came from God, and their special qualities made them God's image, the Israelites had to con-sider human nature very good. This judgment, in fact, provoked the myths of the fall, since the evil actions of human beings did not square with what the God of the Exodus and creation must have made them.

The significance of this orientation is not hard to estimate, even when perhaps four thousand years of further experience of nature and humankind have forced biblical religionists to refine it. Those who really have taken the faith of either Abraham or Jesus to heart will look upon creation reverently, seeing it as a cornucopia of divine gifts. When they see creation abused or defaced, they will recoil as though in the presence of sacrilege. For they will have been formed to the instinct that creation simply does not belong to human beings as theirs to use however they wish. The readings of Genesis 1:28 ("And God blessed them, and God said to them, 'Be fruitful and multiply, and fill the earth and subdue it; and have dominion over the fish of the sea and over the birds of the air and over every living thing that moves upon the earth'") that encourage the careless use of nature will jar mature adherents of biblical religion thoroughly, even when such readings come from enthusiastic Christian evolutionists or popes writing encyclicals on human labor. The meaning of whatever exists ultimately refers us to the mysterious source of all that exists. The fact that something exists should create in us a respect that prejudices us in favor of what will support that creature's continuance in being and flourishing.

Religious traditions other than the bibilical ones have frequently developed this interest more fully. For example, the Hindu notion of *ahimsa* or non-injury finally reposes, for a developed philosophical position such as Advaita Vedānta, on the presence of the holy Brahman, or ultimate reality, to everything that has being. Less metaphysically and more aesthetically, the classical Taoists sometimes spoke of the flow of nature as something that one should respect to the point of sacrifice. Many Buddhists, shaped by both Indian and East Asian culture, have followed an equivalent ethical system, as the five most general precepts of *sila* suggest.

In Christianity it has been the philosophers and mystics who have gone to the crux of the significance of creation, in the process usually joining biblical stimuli to Greek insights. For example, reading Exodus 3:14 under the influence of a philosopher such as Parmenides, they could wonder at existence: the way that whatever is has stepped forth from (*ex sistere*) the void of nothingness. By the time of Aquinas this strand of existentialism, muted by the Aristotelian focus on form but abetted by the Platonic sense of participation, had produced an understanding of creation according to which the nature of God was pure existence and the inmost reality of any creature was the ongoing grant of being that God was making to it. Indeed, were God not to conserve the creature in being and concur in the creature's actions, there would be no non-divine being, having, or doing. The mystics, among whom we should number Aquinas himself, put all this in more precisely religious language when they spoke of their utter dependence on the Creator. John of the Cross, for example, used the backdrop of Thomistic metaphysics to intimate that the dark night of the soul was teaching the creature the bedrock truth of its nothingness apart from God. This annihilation was of course considered positive—an invitation to a realism that sinful people never received. Yet the harrowing quality of the mystic's negative experiences (I continue to say nothing about sin but am still speaking only of creaturehood) made overwhelming the grandeur of God and the contingent, non-necessary quality of both creation and the thematic "God saw that it was good."

Modern Western philosophy received this tradition through the work of Leibnitz and Heidegger, who said the fundamental question is why there is something rather than nothing. For the person of biblical faith there is something only because God chose to communicate outside of the divinity. God need not have created, just as God need not have redeemed. For there to be creation is grace, in the sense of an unowed divine generosity. In fact, as many very holy adherents of biblical religion have concluded, everything is grace. If we go to the foundations of ourselves or nature, we realize that the entirety of us could not be. This realization does not, of course, absolve us from dealing with the further question of why so much that is is twisted. We still have the problems of evil and theodicy. But as long as we remember the depths to which Genesis and the biblical mystics point, we will not deal with any part of creation casually. Each creature will evoke something of the divine mystery or fontal fullness of being, so each creature will solicit our reverence.

· SIN ·

The second Christian orientation that we must consider is sin. It is the negative player in the drama of creation and human history. Sin itself, most Christian theologians have said one way or another, is nothing positive or rational, but a privation of the good order that ought to exist. Specifically, it is the privation of the good moral order that ought to exist—the order fashioned by human beings' free choices. A physical evil such as cancer or destructive earthquake is not sin, because there is nothing moral or freely chosen about it. (I bracket the question of how to regard the Creator's responsibility for natural evils.) When we speak of sin, therefore, we speak of a disorder or a missing of the mark or a lovelessness that Christian theology has said only human beings (and angels) can produce.

The biblical instinct is that sin comes from a forgetfulness of God or an aversion from God. God, the creative mystery and redemptive force that Judaism and Christianity consider the source of human beings' order, has made the creatures who exist in the divine image capable of rejecting their source. We have a significant measure of freedom, and when we abuse it we sin. The results of our sins are both personal and social. Just as we don't come into being apart from other people and natural relationships, so we don't do either good or evil without impinging on other people and the ecosphere. Put in this rather bald way, the propositions may appear either aggressive or banal, but in fact they sharpen the assumptions that humanity at large acts upon every day.

We assume, for example, that children have responsibilities to their parents and parents have responsibilities to their children. We assume that individuals will enter into agreements with others regarding their labor and the provision of services. Nowadays we realize that housing developments or new industrial tracts are not built in a vacuum but occur in a sensitive ecosphere, so we require environmental impact studies. Even religion, which might at first glance appear the most private or solitary of personal activities, turns out to be unremittingly social, as the churches and synagogues dotting the land testify. So the order or disorder of an individual's spirit bears consequences to the rest of reality at large. The ignorance of God or aversion from God that the Bible considers the core of sin is very much everybody's business.

One sees this in the codes of biblical religion, both the decalogue of the Torah and the new, twofold commandment of Jesus. Both begin with the relationship between God and creatures but then move to relationships among creatures. As Jesus boiled it all down, the two great religious imperatives are to love God with our whole mind, heart, soul, and strength, and to love our neighbors as ourselves. To fail these imperatives, and so sin, is to close ourselves off from God, refusing to love the creative mystery from which we derive, and to close ourselves off from our neighbors, refusing to love those who are our equals in being images of this Creator.

There is no sense pretending that, in the present context, I don't see these first two orientations of Christian religion as entirely germane to the matter of abortion. Just as the bold strokes of any inference from the doctrine of creation that I would consider logical and valid run to the conclusion that one must greatly reverence all human life, so the bold strokes of a similar inference from the doctrine of sin run to the conclusion that not loving one's human neighbors

—indeed, terminating their lives—is abhorrent. At the least, therefore, the practice of abortion has a great burden of proof laid upon it. To judge it compatible with a Christian faith oriented by the biblical and traditional doctrines of creation and sin, one has to surmount a high wall of unlikelihood.

The doctrine of sin has of course sponsored further refinements, and some of those most relevant to our present discussion concern how one ought to consider human nature. To what extent does the doctrine of human sinfulness, which certainly seems to have solid empirical grounds in the disorder and man-made suffering that have consistently tainted human history, imply that one must restrain the refrain about the goodness of creation in the case of human beings? The Christian traditions have somewhat differed in the tenor of their response to this question, Protestants classically discuss the corruption of human nature, and Catholics and Eastern Orthodox speak of a darkening of the mind and weakening of the will, but as a summary statement few would dispute that Christianity supports a proper hermeneutics of suspicion. In other words, we are wise to keep a close check on human motivation, both our own and that of other people. The wry observation that human beings are the only species that can blush, or that needs to, applies. We all do well to practice a constant examination of conscience. If we do, we will not be surprised that many opinions and actions of others seem self-serving rather than objective (let alone conformed to the selfless agape of Christ), because we will have met such egocentricity within. As the great theologian Pogo put it: "We have met the enemy and they are us."

A hermeneutic of suspicion should not, to be sure, rule the day or take away a proper openness and positive predisposition. People should be assumed to be well-motivated, as they should be assumed to be intelligent, until they show themselves to be something contrary. Yet only by burying our heads in the sand will we be able to avoid the judgment that sometimes, indeed often, people are badly motivated, just as sometimes, indeed often, people show themselves stupid. And it will only require a slight development of this observation to add that distorted motivation may increase to the degree that people have a strong interest, whether an advantage to gain or a disadvantage to avoid. This, too, will not be the whole story, since interest or involvement also can be a source of deepened understanding. But it will provide properly cautionary maxims to guide our praxis.

Again, to bring this to bear on abortion, one has to take sinful disorders seriously into account when evaluating different positions, and philosophies that do not provide for human sinfulness—or for the regular effort to grow in self-knowledge that the doctrine of sin has made a prominent goal of Christian spirituality—will appear seriously deficient. Self-interest may certainly direct opponents of abortion as much as advocates, but any campaign that depicts one side or the other as above using abortion to achieve political goals should be held suspect. Relatedly, efforts to suggest that abortion is a peculiarly religious matter, or that the only parties to the abortion debate with a special bias are Catholic Christians and others possessing clearly articulated beliefs about the ultimate reference of human life to a Creator, should be dismissed as bogus or as deliberate tactics of manipulation.

Perhaps I should confess at this point that the book on abortion that has most impressed me is John T. Noonan, Jr.'s *A Private Choice*,[1] of which I shall speak more later. Here what comes to mind is the theological supplement that the traditional biblical doctrine of sin provides. What Noonan lays out in historical, legal, and philosophical terms the Christian theologian must subsume into the higher (to the theologian's mind) viewpoint afforded by creation, sin, and grace. Insofar as Noonan's analysis reveals that the movements that led to the Supreme Court's establishment of the right to abortion in 1973 (*Roe* v. *Wade*) were terribly mottled by misrepresentation, prejudice, and a dubious overthrow of prior legal tradition, he writes almost a case study in the social dynamics of sin. Some of the parties to these movements no doubt collaborated and planned carefully, but more appear simply to have acted out their own (religious) disorder.

· GRACE ·

Complementary to the Christian doctrine of sin is the doctrine of grace, and the hallmark of the New Testament's view of grace is Paul's conviction that where sin abounded grace has abounded the more (Romans 5:20). The first inference that Christianity has drawn from this view is that, despite sin, human life and creation as a whole continue to be cause for blessing God. The second inference is that the salvation from sin that God's free favor has made available is a further mercy and cause for blessing the Creator. If God has continued to love us even when we have been sinners, then our lives have an unconditionally solid foundation.

The third and to my mind most amazing dimension of grace is the share in the divine life that God's favor has made possible. When we open ourselves to the divine mystery and return love for love, we receive much more than a deepening and healing into right order. We receive as well the very life of Father-Son-Spirit that Christian religion says is the inmost nature of the Creator. This does more than burnish the image of God described in the creation account of Genesis. It takes human nature up into something eye had not seen or ear had not heard, something it had not entered the human heart to conceive. Whatever special dignity among all creatures human beings had through their reflective consciousness has increased exponentially. For now we participate in the deathless divine love and may anticipate the heavenly fulfillment promised in Christ's resurrection. This resurrection, along with the pledge of the Holy Spirit moving in believers' hearts, has traditionally shifted theologians' focus from the healing powers of grace to its powers of elevation. The mercy of God is not limited to the temporal restorations to health that the Spirit constantly labors to provide. It elevates human consciousness and dignity to the glory of the divine life itself—the splendor of the biblical *Shekinah* and aura of the Johannine Christ making his high priestly prayer to the Father before mounting the cross (in triumph).

Creation, sin, and grace therefore considerably stretch the anthropology or understanding of human nature that rules in most secular debates. By consensus (usually tacit but sometimes express), neither the gratuity of all creatures' existence, nor the twistedness of the human heart sealed off from God, nor the glorious (strictly supernatural) destiny awaiting the images of the Trinitarian God, are allowed entry. This consensus has its good reasons, of course, since a pluralistic society has to limit the influence of convictions peculiar to given minority groups. Such reasons have less force when discussing traditional Christian convictions in the context of the history or present culture of the United States, where the majority world view has been mainstream biblical Christianity, but even here divergent minorities have their rights. When it comes to discussing how Christians ought most prudently to engage in pluralistic politics, therefore, the height and depth of Christian anthropology may have to be somewhat bracketed. Right now, however, our task is to appreciate the view of human existence that Christianity, left to exfoliate all its instincts about grace, tends to develop. To say the least, that view of human existence makes each person very precious. Mother Teresa of Calcutta may seldom discuss grace as healing and elevating, but she clearly senses the respect and love for even the most wretched human being that traditional Christianity should sponsor.

This said, I must of course start to deal with the many lets and hindrances which human sin and finitude place on the ideals of Christian anthropology. What happens, practically, to the doctrines of creation, sin, and grace when many people are ignorant, warped by heredity and environment, stuck at the stage of the law of the jungle? In Platonic terms, how does one legislate and control when only the few are composed of precious metals and the many seem made of rusty brass? Has Christianity not compromised significantly in matters of war and the exploitation of nature? Do its colonialism, racism, sexism, clericalism and other defects not force us to a thorough criticism of its doctrines?

We should indeed criticize all of Christian doctrine and pay more attention to what Christians have done than to what they have said. (We should also treat all other religions and secular positions similarly.) So doing, what we will find is a very mixed bag. Partly because of Christians' own shortcomings and partly because of qualities of the human condition (finitude and sin) that the Christian doctrines elucidate very well, Christian ethicians have had to deal with murder, incest, rape, theft, war, lying, and all the other familiar expressions of human disorder. This dealing has inevitably been a blend of induction and deduction, of common sense and theory. The central reference point to which Christian ethical theory as a whole has tended to return, however, has been the dignity of the human person.[2] Coming from the divine Creator, redeemed by the divine Son, and destined for the divine eternity, the human person has been considered something sacred. Thus to violate the human person ethically, one has had to carry a great burden of proof.

In the traditional teachings of Catholic Christianity about war, for example, the conditions under which one could claim to be waging war justly have been stringent indeed. The great burden of proof has been against war and those who would initiate it. In thinking about attacks on individual people that would terminate life, such as murder on the streets or mercy killings in hospitals, the burden of proof has rested completely with the executioner. True enough, discussion of euthanasia has suggested scenarios in which simply physical existence would not be the predominant good, just as liberation theology has verged on scenarios in which the *violencia blanca* of systemic poverty, torture, and oppression would be a worse evil than revolutionary killing. But even in these cases, which legitimately ask the Christian ethical tradition to grow more sophisticated and better able to handle a very complicated and tangled human reality, reverencing human life and personhood has commanded central attention. No creature on whom God has lavished the love of Christ and the offer of divine life ought ever to be treated casually, let alone brutally or destructively. At most, the Christian ethical tradition has felt that one might repulse unjust aggressors or people trying to perpetrate evil. This was supposed to be done reluctantly, and with no more counter-violence or destruction than was necessary to thwart such evil doers.

Applied to abortion, which has appeared on the lists of grave sins from the time of early Christianity, the assumption was that new human life in the womb was sufficiently human to share in the dignity, respect, and rights owed a human person. Sometimes sophisticatedly, more frequently not, the Christian instinct was historically that life in the womb—certainly from the time of quickening and probably from conception—was but the first phase in the life process of a new human person. As such it had dignity and a set of rights independent of its mother. To terminate the life of the fetus was to try to ruin something God-given, as was infanticide. Historians of the Christian attitudes toward abortion have certainly shown us exceptions or qualifications to this general instinct, but in my view they have only confirmed that overall Christianity has put the great burden of proof on those who would kill life in the womb. At least as much as perpetrators of murder on the street or destruction through warfare, abortionists have been cast as people apparently running counter to the order of creation and grace. With street-murderers and warmongers, they have been cast as sinners—people in revolt against God. The life in the womb being considered innocent (no evil aggressor against the mother), destructive action against it could no more be called holy than destructive action against innocent populations could be called holy war (the perversions of which, in Judaism, Christianity, and Islam alike, are another sorry chapter in the history of sin). Summarily, then, the feminist jibe that "if men had to carry children abortion would be a sacrament" is not only sexist but full of anti-Catholic Christian bigotry. Any who would proffer it seriously have closed themselves to Christian grace.

· LOVE ·

The last of the orientations I think we should take from Christian theory is love. Its universal relevance comes through in the traditional epitome of Christian political wisdom: "In necessary things, unity; in doubtful things, liberty; and in all things, charity." For present purposes, the relevance of love or charity minimally means not putting sinners of any stripe, including abortionists, outside the pale of divine grace. We have all sinned and fallen short of God's glory. In all of our cases God alone descries the heart and can fully render just judgment. Christian ethicians and politicians have not always remembered these calls to charity and humility, nor have they always exhibited the good will or effort to understand others' viewpoints that these suggest. Maximally, the love at the center of Christian religion ought to move its adherents to labor mightily to help people who are brought into destructive situations, and lessen their need to contribute yet more destruction or sin.

Third, the love that Christianity has associated with the Holy Spirit can be dexterous and subtle, and can deal with a complicated human reality sophisticatedly. Ultimately it does slip out of sight into the mysteriously simple divine love, but in time or history it can be graduated, diverse, and shaded. One starts to suggest this when calling on the Christian dictum that we are to hate the sin but love the sinner. Not the most happily phrased bit of advice, this dictum soon cedes to other qualifications to absolutism, and then finally to a virtual silence that waits upon concrete cases. In the final analysis only the wise or prudent or mature person is competent to sift out the many relevant factors and discern what Christian instinct makes of the whole. Such a person knows that ethical theory and tradition are instrumental rather than absolute. They are letters meant to serve or express the Spirit, not substitutes for the Spirit.

What might an ethically mature Christian, animated by a love not at all feigned, think about the current abortion controversy? First, that both Christian and secular traditions of free responsible speech ought to continue. We need a full exchange of scholarship and ideas if we are to rightly estimate the impact of such new factors as women's liberation and biomedical advancements. This ethically mature person would probably criticize efforts to muzzle or discredit Catholic ethicians, such as Daniel Maguire, who have urged changes in the traditional condemnation of abortion. We need all the light that intelligence, faith, and good will (qualities Maguire has in abundance) can shed. To forbid such a person access to Catholic university platforms calls into question the possibility of a genuine Catholic intellectualism. To withdraw access to speak on ethical topics other than abortion after invitations have been tendered is, as Maguire himself has put it, to engage in a sort of "shunning" more associated with narrow Christian sects than with Catholicism.

The love associated with maturity in the Spirit ought also to enable us to make useful distinctions between abortion and contraception and so further remove the legitimacy of using abortion as a contraceptive. I find it instructive, for example, that public opinion, both inside Catholic Christianity and outside in American culture at large, is so much more negative about abortion than about contraception. Here again a full discussion would involve many distinctions, and certainly any ethician of substance is not going to make public opinion probative (even if we could determine it wholly accurately). Further, what contraception is "artificial" and what "natural" is hard to say. In my perception, however, the far greater abhorrence people show for abortion than for contraception derives from the fact that contraception seems responsible and abortion seems irresponsible. One can combine contraception with a commitment to a human fruitfulness and a reverence for life (especially for the "quality" of human life, about which we must speak more later), especially when this contraception follows the body's own rhythms and intrudes nothing chemical that is potentially dangerous. Even when one is speaking of something as artificial as a diaphragm or a condom, however, the interference with either the partners' expression of love or the partners' overall commitment to procreation seems minimal. Sensing this, the majority of people reject both abortion and conservative religious positions such as that of Pope John Paul II (which would demand that each act of sexual love be open to procreation) as irrational extremes. With a minimal amount of foresight and interference with nature and personhood, and with a major set of positive benefits (to population control, family flourishing, and conscience), a proper use of contraceptive techniques seems to serve the prudent love by which the Holy Spirit would keep human beings both well-rooted in the essenial theological virtues and able to handle shifting accidental matters. By contrast, abortion appears as a failure to plan, reverence life, or submit oneself to the bigger picture that God, nature, and society compose.[3]

The God that Christians find best intimated by love is the main artist of the reality that ethical human actions subserve, and so it is consoling indeed to recall the Johannine conviction that even when our hearts condemn us God is greater than our hearts (I John 3:20). In fact, the only unforgiveable sin is shutting one's heart against the Holy Spirit and so refusing to admit the divine transcendence and the objective order of creation that it has established. An experienced or mature Christian ethician certainly is not going to rush in with this negative judgment whenever someone confesses having committed or secured an abortion. Only the abortionist who shuts out the divine mystery, love, and order is a strong candidate for the deepest circle of sinners in hell, those who have completely disdained the love that the Spirit would pour forth in their hearts. Others, who appear confused, divided, and reluctant, may have seriously failed the divine standards, but God certainly remains greater than their sorry hearts and able to forgive them—seventy times seven, if need be.

God also certainly remains greater than our ability to discern the divine ways of salvation and competent to render justice to the fetal victims of abortion. We shall never have certitude about salvation into heavenly fulfillment, because such salvation depends on God's free grant of the love that is inseparable from the divine mystery. All of our speculations about heaven, limbo, infant baptism, and the rest remain just that: speculations. Christian faith would seem seriously to fail, however, when it equates abortion with the utter frustration of God's intentions. Abortion may in fact be an attempt, deliberate or regretted, to frustrate or contradict what we perceive to be the patterns of salvation, but, as the Buddhists are fond of saying, the ultimate reality is "skillful in means to save." God might appear directly to embryonic human life and give it a chance to choose for or against the divine will. God might consider it the equal of those who have lived a long life but not suffered a like brutality, the way that the generous owner of the vineyard considered the laborers hired last the equals of those hired first (Matthew 20: 1–16). We simply don't know, so we must reason from surer convictions about the divine love. Certainly God loves everything to which divinity grants existence, life, and breath. Certainly this love fulfills whatever we would consider "justice" and then some. Abortion therefore is never greater than God or God's heart.

·7·

FEMINIST THEORY

· EQUALITY ·

Parallel to the help that a recollection of Christian theory may bring
is help from a recollection of feminist theory. In the following description of the feminist outlook, as with the prior review of the
Christian outlook, I am attempting a general or centrist view. As
actually lived out, Christianity has many different outlooks, theories, theologies, and ethical options. From New Testament times to
the present, different Christian groups have conceived faith in
Christ differently. Those who would stress pluralism rather than
unity or even coherence therefore have some good data on their
side. The same is true of those who would stress the pluralism within feminism. There is no one feminist theory, politics, or set of ethical opinions. Nonetheless, just as I find it helpful to express my
sense of the background or orientation that Christian faith gives to
the abortion controversy, so I find it helpful to express my sense of
feminist allegiance. To my mind the first conviction requisite for
genuine feminism, and the one most important throughout, is the
equality that women have with men in possessing humanity or
human nature.

Genesis 1:27 can be cited in support of women's equality with
men in possessing human nature (or the image of God): "So God
created man in his own image, in the image of God he created him;
male and female he created them." Still, the problems of the generic
"man" (and of the masculine pronoun for God) mute the force of
the last phrase. In addition, large groups within the feminist camp
are uncomfortable citing the Bible as it now stands (some groups

97

will cite it in revised form, whether that of Elizabeth Cady Stanton or some other feminist), so the arguments for women's equal humanity tend to come from other sources.

Probably representative of the mainstream of current feminist thought is the following statment that occurs early in the introductory textbook on women's studies that has been produced by the Women's Studies Collective of Hunter College:

> The attitude, however subtle, that permeates definitions of women is the view of woman as "the other." Thus, women have been defined as "not men." This is evident in the emphasis in research on the differences between women and men. In this way, women have been defined by comparison: *more* frivolous, *less* rational, *closer* to nature, or *more* nurturing, for example. Women have been defined by our endocrine and reproductive systems—that which makes us *different* from men. Men have been viewed as the norm, and women as a deviation from that norm. What is identified as "male" has been viewed as "ideal," and thus "male" characteristics have been highly valued. By comparison, women's characteristics have been devalued because we have been viewed as defective or incomplete males, less than "ideal," and even less than human.[1]

If one either assumes or argues that women in fact are as fully human as men, the imbalance implied in the paragraph cited above becomes obvious. Obvious, as well, is the oppression, now slight and now gross, that we shall study in the next section. Women have been the second sex, the underside of history, the numerical majority with a minority of the power and prestige. The equality assumed or argued for by most women (although not necessarily by most texts in women's studies) is just that: equal humanity. It wants the redefinition of homo sapiens so that this term means what the last phrase of Genesis 1:27 says: the creation (whether by God or through evolution or from the two conjoined) of our species makes femaleness and maleness dead level in their necessity and in their contribution to survival and prosperity.

This equality, however, does not mean sameness. Sexual differentiation, from the outset, obviates that. Probably the majority of professors of women's studies, wanting to concentrate on what women have done and been throughout history, don't even bother to articulate their acceptance of difference. That might get them back into a comparative mode, and so return them close to the spontaneous assumption that masculine ways, standing over against feminine ways, are the human norm. Men of course turn up in studies of women's history and reality, sometimes in major roles, but the focus remains women's half of the human reality. A sensitive novelist such as Mary Gordon often conveys the "feel" of this half of the human reality better than the writers of textbooks.[2]

Some feminists, however, shoot for something that they consider higher than equality. To their mind, women are superior to men—whether biologically, ethically, or just in terms of interest—and so equality, androgyny, partnership and other ways of expressing the "male and female he created them" will not do. The few members of this party radical enough to want to withdraw as much as possible from men in effect try to rewrite human biology and history. Perhaps Mary Daly, whose revolt is in part from Catholic Christianity, is a good example of the assets and liabilities of this position.[3]

On the one hand, the sharpness of Daly's anger and alienation from male-dominated culture makes her writing creative, at times brilliant. She sees the evils that sexism has wrought and brings them home to the reader unforgettably. On the other hand, where is one to go with sexual separatism of any marked degree? Daly has tried to keep men from attending her classes at Boston College, but hardly to the credit of feminism. She has tried to ignore the many instances of masculine virtue or of heterosexual love, but hardly to the credit of her realism. And the anger or even hatred that laces her work, even when one makes large provision for a basis in shattered idealism and hurt, is bound to chill those who feel, whether from Christian conviction or just plain human experience, that love is the only force capable of healing the depth of humanity's fractures.

Consequently, feminists who deny equality or refuse to make equality the watchword of their movement tend greatly to reduce their influence. To the majority of their fellow human beings, women and men, they are flying in the face of simple reality and objectivity. The brilliance of their flights of rhetoric, imagination, and historical reconstruction notwithstanding, women's superiority to men or difference in kind seldom wins acceptance. On the contrary, striving to realize politically, culturally, religiously and in all other ways women's equality to men in human nature strikes the vast majority of people as the agenda that realism recommends.

I have used this agenda in the first part of this book, arguing in diverse ways that the refusal of equality that Catholic Christianity's denial of women's aptness for sacramental orders epitomizes brands Catholic Christianity sexist and so in need of conversion, penance, and behavioral change. To my mind equality is more than purely tactical, however. To my mind the heterosexuality of homo sapiens is one of those (relatively few) objective "givens" that signal the presence of the divine Creator. One may call that divine Creator Father or Mother, but by any name the source of our two-sexed human reality, from which we derive both some of our strongest love and all of our procreation, is incontrovertibly present in our male-femaleness. The implications we should draw from this concerning homosexuality are another task for another day. Suffice it for me to say now that I have no quarrel with a homosexuality, male or female, that retains kindly contact with humanity as a whole. If a person must say, in all honesty and conscientiousness, that he or she seems consistently oriented toward members of his or her own sex, I must say, in return, "God love you." The implication I see in this traditional saying is that God made any of us as we, in our most honest moments, define ourselves. I would reject any definition that set any of us outside the whole of us, or that spurned the call to honesty and love that I find constitutive of human be-ing. Granted this, however, I find homosexuality, like heterosexuality, something that must be judged by the fruits which it grows. I have seen it grow good fruits and bad fruits, just as with heterosexuality. I have seen nothing in it that says it necessarily places gay people below straight people in the evaluations of God. As with maleness and femaleness, I think that the sanest judgment first thinks in terms of equal humanity.

· OPPRESSION ·

By modern standards of equality, women are oppressed—held below parity—in most of today's societies, and women have been oppressed throughout recorded history. If one uses such criteria as equal economic opportunity, equal access to political power, and prestige or status according to society's definitions of success and wisdom, women come out the underlings. Thus Vern Bullough's still serviceable history of attitudes toward women is well titled *The Subordinate Sex.*[4]

The judgment does not change dramatically when the topic is the status of women in religious societies. One who reads a work like Geoffrey Parrinder's *Sex in the World Religions*[5] with today's sensibilities finds that feminine manifestations of power inextricably woven through numinous reality have regularly held less prestige and more danger than male manifestations. My own study, *Women and World Religion*,[6] argues to the same conclusion, as do studies such as Falk and Gross's *Unspoken Worlds*,[7] which concentrate on letting women from non-biblical cultures speak in their own voice. Again and again these windows onto women's historical experience show us a culture in which it is simply assumed that men will run things and women will obey. Again and again women have less voice, more suffering, and less share in the analogies by which the people speak about God. Some feminist historians argue that this was not the case in prehistoric eras. Remnants of a Great Goddess religion or a matriarchal society lead them to think that earlier the deity was pictured as more feminine than masculine and that much of the tribal power reposed in women's hands. Even if these theories come to win general acceptance, however, the historical record will remain besmirched. Thus today's feminists will continue to feel justified in thinking of women as an oppressed sex that must fight to overthrow longstanding patterns of domination.

This judgment is nearly inseparable from the assumption that women are as human as men, when that assumption combines with an unblinking look at how women have actually been treated throughout history. Even when one grows sufficiently sophisticated to provide for all of the informal power, influence, and success that women certainly have achieved, the established patterns remain the enemy. This is the case, for a quite relevant example, with Catholic Christianity. No one studying Catholic Christian theology or history with an unprejudiced eye could conclude that women did not have as much chance for salvation as men. Nonetheless, from very early on Christianity agreed to treat women within the patriarchal assumptions of the Jewish and Graeco-Roman cultures, and so women did not have equal access to church power and dignity. Women could be saints, but they could not lead the church or represent the parental God as directly as men. The most honored woman, the Virgin Mary, was greatly cherished, but almost all the strictly divine aspects of church life were cast in male terms. Indeed, femaleness became a debit after the rise of Christian monasticism and celibacy, because women more obviously became impediments to what was conceived as the spiritual ideal. Then the misogynistic strains of the New Testament itself, as perhaps most offensively summarized in I Timothy 2: 11–15, seemed to support women's living under a cloud of suspicion.

Let us recall this classical text, for it bears on abortion as well as women's general status in Christian estimate: "Let a woman learn in silence with all submissiveness. I permit no woman to teach or to have authority over men; she is to keep silent. For Adam was formed first, then Eve; and Adam was not deceived, but the woman was deceived and became a transgressor. Yet woman will be saved through bearing children, if she continues in faith and love and holiness, with modesty." First, the text could be cited by those who wished to keep the liturgy and catechetical office of the church a male preserve, and by those who wanted women barred from church authority (at least over males) generally. Second, the text makes maleness the prime instance of humanity and suggests that femaleness is a tagalong. Third, the text lays most of the responsibility for human fallenness, with its consequents of suffering, alienation, and unhappiness, on the femaleness symbolized by Eve. Fourth and last, the text would nearly define religious womanhood through childbearing, suggesting that women need only fulfill this natural task with proper faith, love, holiness, and modesty to be saved.

Not all Christian theologians or laypeople read this text literally or to women's full detriment, of course, but all were at least subtly influenced by it. Fathers of the church such as Augustine, Chrysostom, Tertullian, and Jerome all used it and other bits of biblical patriarchalism to denigrate women and femaleness. It played in the background of the Catholic Christian view that the two main ends of marriage were procreation and the remedy of concupiscence, and that procreation clearly was primary. As a result, the women whose lives were shaped by Catholic Christianity were oppressed: considered less estimable than men and formed by their sex as men were not formed or limited by theirs.

Feminists approaching matters of sexual morality therefore should be excused many of their suspicions of religious spokespersons. Both inside Christianity and outside in other traditions, mainstream opinion has not supported women's equality. Women have borne the burden of securing a proper control of sexual passion, even when much of the cultural symbolism branded the female as more impetuous and unreliable than the male. If a woman was judged unchaste it redounded much more to her discredit than a similar judgment would have afflicted a male. Menstruation often had the connotation of being dirty, polluting, and unmentionable, and the remains of the blood-taboo spilled some of this negativity over onto birth. Thus women were to be "churched" after childbirth, in a rite that was a cleansing as well as a celebration. At times popular opinion held that women should not receive communion while menstruating, and that couples should abstain from sexual relations during penitential periods such as Lent. This latter opinion of course carried a negative judgment on the sexual activity of men as well as women, but on the whole it amplified the monastic tendency to think that if men were not dragged down into sensuality by women they could live much closer to the angels. Women—close to nature, blood, children, and all the messy rest—therefore became the enemies of such higher things as intellectualism, celibacy, and full-time devotion to religious service.

Abortion was scarcely mentioned in such a catalogue of the reasons why it would be proper to consider women the subordinate sex. Theologians tended to think of it as occurring alongside witchcraft and the occult arts they feared women might be indulging.[8] For although childbirth was a female preserve when it came to feelings of taboo, the objective importance of procreation led male theologians and church leaders to legislate about its moral dimensions. At no time did the moral theology of either the church or Western society at large think that women ought to have the first, last, or even equal word about the control of their own fertility. To many contemporary feminists this is a central symbol of the oppression that women have suffered. From birth control to rape, women have regularly had their own sexuality, and so much of their own personhood, controlled by others. The battle for the right to abort unwanted children therefore can seem the key struggle in the fight for overall equality. If one believes that the fetus is not a person or an entity sufficiently human to entitle it to ordinary human rights, abortion on women's demand can seem a great advance into enlightenment and sexual equality.

· AUTONOMY ·

Autonomy was a watchword of the eighteenth century Enlightenment, which continues to exert great philosophical influence today. The notion, probably most thoroughly developed by Kant, that modern maturity demanded putting aside heteronomous reliance on outside authorities, whether of church or state, contributed greatly to the anthropologies of Jefferson, Franklin, Madison, and the other framers of American constitutional philosophy. Although John Locke was no doubt a more direct influence than Kant, the Kantian stress on individual conscience (with or without reference to the Protestant Reformers who spoke similarly) helped to distance American religious and political thought from that of Catholic Christianity. In my opinion, this produced a dialectical situation, one in which both partners had something to learn.

Catholic Christianity certainly had something to learn from the Protestant Reformation and the Enlightenment about the consequences of (Catholic Christianity's own doctrine of) the centrality of personal conscience. Institutional Christianity had grown to the point where heteronomy did prevail in many ethical situations and people were trying to cede their inalienable responsibilities for their actions to a church authority or moral code. Church authority itself too often rode roughshod over individual conscience, expecting people to take all its pronouncements without criticism—often without even reflective thought. The great institutional virtue was obedience (never the highest virtue, when a religion is fully vital), and the shepherds definitely regarded their charges as sheep. One finds this attitude in such recent popes as Gregory XVI and Pius X: "No one can deny that the Church is an unequal society in which God destined some to be governors and others to be servants. The latter are the laity; the former, the clergy"; "Only the college of pastors have the right and authority to lead and govern. The masses have no right or authority except that of being governed, like an obedient flock that follows its Shepherd."[9] From those enlightened enough to oppose this classism, whether in the name of New Testament freedom of conscience or in the name of the rationality that modern science had made humanity's great power, Catholic Christianity might have received a wonder purification. As it was Roman Catholicism resisted the lessons of modernity until the Second Vatican Council, and even today many brushfires of opposition still smolder.

The dialectical relationship had a countermovement, however, in which autonomy was challenged to purify its own assumptions and excesses. This challenge was hard to press in the nineteenth century, when science continued to appear an unmixed blessing and revolutionary movements heralded the coming of a classless society. The wars and perversions of the twentieth century, having humbled the hubris of "man come of age," returned considerable perspective as human autonomy disclosed its own set of evils. Not everything bad that happens to us comes from without. The "heart of darkness" that Joseph Conrad and others described functioned in all social systems, socialist as much as capitalist, and only a fool would think that justice, let alone paradise depended on the organization of the state alone. The objective order of nature and divinity did not lose its force simply because human beings decided to declare everything arbitrary or man-made. Societies that claimed to be able to define individualism and justice without referring to this objective order discredited themselves as soon as suffering drove people to take a second look. Thus the slavers of the nineteenth century who campaigned for *Dred Scott* v. *Sanford* were revealed as racist when people in the twentieth century read in that majority opinion that blacks had been regarded by the makers of the Constitution as beings of an inferior order—so inferior that they had no rights which a white man was bound to respect. It remains to be seen whether later generations will view the majority opinion in *Roe* v. *Wade* as similarly limited, but in fact at the time that Justice Blackmun wrote his majority opinion, neither the American people at large nor the laws of most states supported it.

One may argue for a properly Christian autonomy, of course, and I have suggested previously that theologians such as Bernard Lonergan elaborate one most persuasively. In their view, human beings mature by following their drives to transcend themselves. The key drives are those to know and to love, both of which bring us into profound engagement with life's ultimate mystery (the experiential basis for religion). The autonomy most blessed by the Protestant theologian Paul Tillich is actually a "theonomy": a coincidence between what the properly ordered human mind and heart judge real and good and what the divine law prescribes. This may be an asymptotic ideal, best glimpsed in the saints, but it suggests that a fully adequate analysis of human judgment and decision undercuts the dichotomies between objectivity and subjectivity which have plagued modern philosophy. The most responsible and mature people—the most autonomous, in ultimate perspective— find as a matter of fact they are not the sole fashioners of reality, justice, or wisdom. Other beings and forces play in what is actually so, and under pain of violating its own inmost call to light and love, the human self must acknowledge them.

Western law and common sense have both recognized this chastened version of autonomy and so have provided for the social consequences of private acts. Rarely, indeed, has either common law or morality allowed an act to be considered as though the agent were not a thoroughly social being. Both sides of the abortion debate, in fact, have accepted this social dimension to abortion, since both have presented analyses of what abortion has meant in the past, what economic and social consequences it would have today, and how it ought to be approached in a pluralistic society. Similarly, both sides have referred to the objective biological order by trying to take into account the most advanced medical opinions about pre-natal development, genetic disorders, the emotional consequences of rape or incest, and so forth. Indeed, even the objectivity of the transcendent order implied in "God" has received acknowledgment, since both sides have referred to the traditional positions taken down the ages by the religions—Jewish, Protestant, and Catholic—party to the discussion of American morality.

The constitutional position that Congress ought to establish no religion and promote no religious advantage has been thoroughly discussed. Less thoroughly discussed but a potent factor nonetheless have been both sides' assumptions about religion and secularism. For example, many pro-abortionists have promoted the view that only those committed to idiosyncratic religious values oppose the abortion liberty granted by the 1973 Supreme Court decision. This is patently debatable when a majority of Americans describe themselves as adherents of a mainstream or biblically Christian religious position and when at the level of a serious moral option such as abortion the distinction between a "religious" conviction and a "secular" conviction is far from obvious. To state now a judgment I shall develop in the next section: the claim of pro-abortionists that they are more objective and suffer no prejudicial distortions from more-than-rational convictions (such as those that obtain in religion) is self-serving and superficial in the extreme. Whether or not one accepts this challenge to the pro-abortion position held by non-religious debaters, the epistemological force of the assertion should be enough to show that "autonomy" cannot validly be assumed as simple or purely good. Anyone dealing with a choice as momentous as abortion has to define very carefully the "privacy" of the rights of the parties to such a decision.

· SECULARISM ·

Pro-abortionists, to be sure, include religionists as well as non-religionists. Much of my reflection in the next two chapters will be directed toward people of religious conviction, so in this section I want to deal with the force that atheism and agnosticism appear to have intruded into the abortion controversy. On the whole, I consider these two non-religious positions variants of secularism. All names are inadequate when dealing with the ultimate mystery that religionists call God, but practically, if not always finally or idealistically, atheists and agnostics tend to act as though there were no objectively divine order for which they had to provide. By this criterion, of course, many "religionists" show themselves practical atheists or agnostics. However, they do so only at the price of establishing a conflict between what they profess to believe and what they act upon, one which leaves them open to a charge of inconsistency or hypocrisy. Atheists and agnostics who in fact bow to the mysterious love at the core of creation, even when they deny it verbally, present inconsistency in a different garb (one more congenial to me as a religionist, and so one that I would not label hypocritical). Then, I would say, we simply have the common case of people being poor exegetes of their own behavior.

Leaving aside these qualifications, however, let us deal with the generally consistent group of people who make no place for an objective divine order and act as though autonomy meant properly enlightened and social self-interest. It is probably fair to consider the most influential non-religious people who are pro-abortion through this lens. The clarification this brings is that it shows the link between having no instinctive or persistent reference to the divine as the ultimate source of one's moral order, thinking that crucial acts such as abortion are in a quite privatistic sense matters of individual choice, and thinking of the fetus as sub-personal or sub-human: an entity not on the same level of basic humanity as members of the race maturing outside the womb (or even, in some extreme cases, as a destructive intruder or aggressor).

This is all rather speculative, so let me try to make it bear on some specific abortion cases. Those that have made the most impression on me recently came to my attention through Carol Gilligan's study *In a Different Voice*.[10] The vast majority of the women whose moral reasoning was studied by observing their movement through counseling about abortion were, by the author's and perhaps their own admission, ethically and personally underdeveloped. Maturity, responsibility, and success in handling relationships were skills generally missing from their lives. Several were contemplating their second abortion and one or two their third. The men with whom they had involved themselves were a sorry lot, and on the whole the women seemed weak and heteronomous in a pattern fitting the negative female stereotype. One can certainly agree, therefore, that most of them needed a big shot of autonomy and responsibility.

It is one thing to make this statement, however, and another to consider abortion the best expression of a newly developed responsibility, let alone to consider abortion a sort of rite-of-passage to responsibility, autonomy, and maturity. The large number (more than eighty percent) of the women who emerged from their counseling ready and able to obtain an abortion suggests, although it does not prove, that the bias of the counseling was toward solving the problem of an unwanted, inconvenient, or irresponsible pregnancy by aborting the fetal life. I would not want to tax Gilligan with the position that abortion served those women well as a rite-of-passage into maturity, but I have heard such a position set forth in feminist circles: "I finally took responsibility for my own life when I decided to have my abortion."

The index to *In a Different Voice* has no listing for religion, Christianity, or God. This in itself is not probative but it is suggestive. Some of the women studied clearly have religious scruples, and from time to time the moral status of the fetal-life candidate for abortion hovers at the edges of the discussion, but the idea of an objective sacredness to fetal life, granted it by the trans-human Creator, does not figure in the discussions the way it would have to in a truly religious consideration. I conclude, therefore, that the horizon of the book, the study, and the author is secular. The author passes no ultimate or truly moral judgment on the subjects' abortion decisions, whether those have been for or against the termination of fetal life. She certainly does at least imply strongly negative judgments about the moral underdevelopment that played a large role in most of the subjects' having come to the pass of having to make a decision about abortion. But the overall tenor of the book is that the subjects have to choose, and that the fact of their choosing rather than the content of their choice is the thing to focus upon or even celebrate.

Now, there are angles from which a religionist such as I can applaud both the non-judgmental quality of this approach and its laud for making a decision. What I find chilling, and in broader perspective reprehensible, is the result that eventuated in so large a percentage of the decisions. That result could not be qualified as "easy" abortion, in the sense of abortion without emotional or even physical pain. It could be qualified as abortion eased by a disregard or suspension of ultimate religious perspectives. On the whole, I found the horizon of the discussion oppressively this-worldly. It seldom broke out to the realities of sin and grace that might have placed it in a much more powerfully redemptive context. The women being counseled, to be sure, did not need more buckets of guilt dumped on their souls. They did not need the simplistic or fundamentalist sort of religious advice that causes many psychologically oriented counselors, for good reason, to consider "religion" a moral menace. I certainly would not have shown them movies depicting fetuses writhing with pain from abortion procedures or continuing to kick and wiggle with life after they had been evacuated from the womb, nor would I have sent them to a lecture or sermon by Jerry Falwell. I would have spoken about the rights of the prenatal child, the alternatives to abortion, and the religious order alternative to (and to my mind more gracious than) secular systems of evil and good. I would have referred to agencies standing ready to help young women place unwanted children in good homes, and no doubt it would have also made me sad or even angry that these agencies were not more numerous.

The fact is, of course, that often abortion does seem the prudent, simplifying, cleanest solution. The fact is that millions of women every year, in just our country alone, choose it, with more or less reluctance, as a way out of an enormously consequential bind. This solution is immensely simplified when one does not have to deal with the fetus as a human person or with abortion as an act traditionally abhorred by Christians and many other people. When the horizon of the solution is secular—one in which God has no significant role—the choice of abortion is greatly simplified. That the proponents of abortion have recognized this very clearly, and so sought to expand the liberty granted by the Supreme Court in 1973 to the point where any opposition, but especially that based on religious scruples, is branded illegal, immature, un-American, or any of several other varieties of stigma, is argued very effectively by John Noonan. I may be shaped by the anti-Catholicism that Noonan calls ingredient in this effort, finding it another good reason to condemn many of those supporting abortion, but I still find the argument objectively powerful.

This is part of Noonan's description of the dynamic of the abortionists' efforts to expand what they had won in *Roe* v. *Wade*:

> The dynamism of the liberty was to affect every level of government and to alter the distribution of governmental power in American society. At the most fundamental level, judicial interpretation of the liberty was to affect the authority of Congress to appropriate money and to color the Treasury's understanding of its obligations under the Constitution. At the grass-roots level, the liberty was to override the traditional powers of a New England town meeting and to require a town's sense of appropriate community activities to be subordinated to the immune position of an abortion clinic. It was to overturn a school board's control of its teachers and a school board's concern for the teaching of a casual attitude to abortion by the example of a teacher. No corner of the land was to be immune from the liberty's dynamic thrust. The liberty, which could not be confined by geographic or governmental limits, could

not be confined to the womb. The practitioners of personal choice needed to be free not only to kill the unborn but to cause the death of the child already born. Only then would the exercise of the liberty not be "chilled." At a philosophical level, Michael Tooley, a Stanford philosopher, argued that there was no moral distinction between abortion and infanticide: The unsocialized infant outside the uterus was no more a person than his or her brother or sister not yet born.[11]

With secular friends such as this philosopher, feminists of any stripe need no enemies.

·8·

PRUDENTIAL THEOLOGY

· PREVENTION ·

This chapter addresses the position of religious feminists—people who support the equality of women in the context of an objective divine order. It is hard to judge what fraction of either feminists, or women, or the population at large this population includes. On the one hand, the majority of voices one hears in Women's Studies' programs are not religious, and neither are those in the collections of philosophical essays on women and women's issues.[1] On the other hand, large numbers of women, including many dedicated feminists, are strongly committed to spirituality, if not to traditional religion. When taken on a case by case basis, some of this spirituality turns out to be numinous (some is psychological in a reductive sense, not admitting a transcendently divine realm).[2] My audience in this chapter is anyone who sufficiently subscribes to theology—faith seeking understanding—to let the implications of confessing an objectively divine order (i.e., a mystery that transcends secularism) affect ethics and practice. My suspicion is that this is a solid majority of the American population, perhaps two-thirds.

The first desideratum that I find arising from a theological contemplation of abortion is prevention. One wishes to stop the problem before it arises, both because of revulsion at the evil possibilities in abortion and because of the aesthetic appeal of a clean solution. Prevention clearly involves numerous subtopics, some of which will concern us later, but two of the first that come to mind are birth control and sterilization. Each of these has a long history in Catholic Christianity, and so a large body of scholarly literature.

112

The traditional Catholic teaching has treated abortion, birth control, and sterilization in the framework of a moral theology structured by natural law. J. Grundel, writing in an article on birth control for a volume updating traditional Catholic teaching, speedily dismisses the possibility of abortion being a moral choice, and almost as speedily dismisses sterilization: "Killing or aborting the foetus or child have to be rejected as negative methods of birth regulation.... The latter [sterilization] can only be seriously considered as an ultimate possibility when there is an absolute contraindication with regard to new life and where one or both partners have shown intolerance towards other methods of preventing conception."[3] For this author, the permanence of sterilization is the major reason that it is more objectionable than most other methods of preventing conception.

Catholic moral theology has distinguished contraceptive methods into those which are natural and those which are "artificial." This distinction became problematic in the 1960s, but Pope Pius VI's 1968 encyclical *Humanae Vitae* continued to teach in terms of it. Rhythm has been considered natural, and the recent advances in methods for determining the fertile period have convinced many people that rhythm now is a quite practical form of contraception. The pill, the diaphragm, and the condom still labor under the cloud of being considered artificial, although numerous Catholic theologians have judged this designation biologistic, their argument being that just as we may for good reasons alter natural behavior by pills or prostheses in other areas, so we may in the area of birth control. A majority of the Catholic people seems to concur in this judgment. Whether the improvement of rhythm, along with increasing doubts about the safety of chemical treatments such as the pill, will resolve the possible moral conflicts for the majority of Catholic Christians remains to be seen. If that happens, the views of marital intimacy developed by Pope John Paul II in his weekly allocutions may become more persuasive.[4]

Leaving the particulars of the means and ethical niceties to specialists, I would like to use the rest of this section to concentrate on the overall goal. And the first proposition I would like to advance is that feminists would suffer considerably less division over abortion if they could hammer out general agreement that abortion is always a sad, even a tragic option. My sense, in fact, is that ninety percent of American women would concur in this judgment, a solid seventy-five percent being willing to subscribe to it as stated and perhaps another fifteen percent, mainly from more conservative religious circles, wanting more strongly negative language. Perhaps the most leftward fifteen percent within my centrist seventy-five would want to make the point that there can be circumstances in which abortion can seem concretely to be the best option, but these would not make abortion anything positive in its own right. I would guess that only perhaps ten percent of American women would have anything beyond a grudging admission of abortion to offer. This ten percent, moreover, might well treat abortion less on its own terms than as a symbol of women's need to have control of their own lives. The percentage I find waxing enthusiastic about abortion itself therefore is minuscule. Pregnancy and birth are such elementary aspects of womanhood and the survival of the race that just about all human beings first think of them positively.

This is not to say, of course, that every dead rabbit brings a cry of joy. No, because of medical, economic, emotional, or demographic considerations many pregnancies come as rueful, even bitter news. Sometimes this later gives way to a joy that has a strong basis in biological nature, but women and men already hard pressed by family responsibilities can find another pregnancy debilitating. All the more so, of course, can women finding themselves pregnant outside of marriage, to say nothing of women finding themselves pregnant through rape or incest.

If the first word about abortion were to be that we must virtually eliminate it by preventing the conditions from which it spawns, religious feminists would have considerably less quarrel with secular feminists. Granted a coalition to provide the education, birth control, counseling, and alternatives to abortion (especially giving the child up for adoption) that such prevention obviously implies, religious feminists could bracket many of their further convictions about the personhood of the fetus and its attendant rights. Secular feminists, or religious feminists not persuaded of the personhood and rights of the fetus, could for their part have many of their concerns met and many of their alienations assuaged by the sight of conservative religious feminists putting their shoulders to the wheel to save women the trauma of abortion decisions and experiences.

I think this matter of one's commitment to prevention, in fact, could serve as a good touchstone of the genuineness of any person's concern for women's well-being. When it was absent, one would have good grounds for thinking that abortion was in fact serving as a contraceptive, and that people were unwilling to take the trouble to provide alternatives to women's having to undergo something so contrary to their instinctive psychology. Many judges and legislators might fall into this category, along with many bureaucrats in the welfare system. Many doctors and nurses, unfortunately, might fall into this category as well, and in their case the financial benefits of the abortion business would make them further suspect. I doubt that this would be the majority of medical personnel, or even perhaps a large fraction, and I do not want to prejudge judges, lawyers, legislators, and people in the welfare system. All have good reasons (especially the medical personnel) for thinking of their profession as dedicated to saving life and healing. But the controversies about abortion have so muddied the waters that sometimes the bottom line—abortion is the killing of prenatal life—is overlooked. Stressing the prevention of abortion would return us to this bottom line, which in my opinion would be a great injection of sanity. A society that obscures the fact that it is killing its prenatal life on a large scale runs the risk of a large scale psychosis. By evolution and primitive ethical instincts, society is predicated upon generating and protecting life. Abortion, along with making war, is a massive aberration from this instinct of health, a massive failure of rationality.

· SACRIFICE ·

The call to make prevention the first goal of an abortion policy will no doubt not sit well with many pro-abortionists. They are content with a policy that allows abortion on demand and see no pressing reason to alter the status quo. For them the fetus does not have the status of a human person with a human person's attendant rights, and abortion is no violation of an objective divine order. What they would be called upon to sacrifice, then, would be the ignorance of rather obvious biology—the fetus quickly develops into human personhood, if but given minimal care, and for a society to pretend to define personhood apart from this development is capricious or positivistic in the extreme.

The majority of pro-abortionists would also have to give up their pretensions to living in a reality that is, if not completely man-made, without a constraining and encouraging divine mystery. One cannot be sanguine about converting people to this position, of course, but one can rather easily indicate the irrationality of a reductive secularism (more later about a religious viewpoint that stresses the secular). Merely contemplating a creation that human beings did not make, the death that human beings cannot avoid, the love that human beings experience as otherworldly, or the evil that human beings experience as deeply wrong (and so crying out for redress) brings one before what can only be called the mystery of human existence. Not to acknowledge, reverence, and serve this mystery—and live in consequence of its primordiality in our lives—is in my view the most radical irrationality of which human beings are capable. We are not human without this mystery, and from it comes a clear command, repeated in religious tradition after religious tradition, to choose life rather than death. No aberration from this millennial tradition, such as the pathology of Shiite Muslim killers (who know nothing of their own Allah, a God just and merciful), removes the primordiality of the ultimate mystery. In sacrificing their aversion from this God, many pro-abortionists would only be bringing themselves back into the mainstream of mental health.

There is plenty of sacrifice to go around, however, so secular pro-abortionists need not feel singled out for any special hardship. Conservative religionists have to sacrifice their unwillingness to spend the money and time that an effective policy of prevention would entail. They have to drop their prudish opposition to sex education, their niggling over small matters of contraceptive means, and their sense of superiority to women who get themselves in trouble. In the specifically Catholic case, the need to keep current teaching in line with prior teaching has to be dethroned, so that people take priority over papal privileges. Just as it is a scandal that papal prerogatives have been a huge roadblock to ecumenical reunion, and just as it is a scandal that clerical privileges keep the female half of the species from equal citizenship in Catholic Christianity, so it is also a scandal that supposed doctrinal consistency should have outweighed the advice of the majority of experts convened to study birth control and that the 1968 encyclical *Humanae Vitae* should have only exacerbated the problem. By the same token, it is also imperative that Catholic Christian leaders deal with the very real problems of world population growth. While I sympathize with their position that existing has a certain priority over existing well, I think their practical disregard of the misery of the millions now suffering in overpopulated countries like India and overpopulated cities like Mexico City, and of the projections of more than 10 billion people worldwide in the mid-twenty-first century, is scandalous. There comes a point at which matters of scale ought to influence prudential theology. We have reached that point in today's demographic projections, and for it not to be reforming papal policy about birth control nearly destroys the credibility of papal claims to be serving a God who cares preferentially for the poor.

There is still more sacrifice needed, and the two final kinds that I shall consider are those which directly affect pregnant women and American culture at large. Taking the latter first, I would say that an ethic premised on defending and reverencing life and opposing death demands quite a thorough overhaul of our current culture. Abortion and the building of military weapons are perhaps the most prominent facets, but our materialism and self-indulgence also play important roles. As our abortion policies and practices show us to be a people in revolt from the standards of Deuteronomy's two ways of life and of death, so do our policies and practices in military matters. In both areas we have abandoned common sense and gotten ourselves into such spiritual convolutions that our deterrence policy is based upon mutual assured destruction and our health care has a huge industry concerned with killing fetuses.

We could not do this without having become people bent on seizing the day and ignoring posterity. We do not do this in isolation from our contempt for poor people and our exploitation of the peasant population of South America. The logic of the American Catholic bishops' recent pastoral letters on the economy and peacemaking is impeccable. A consistent ethic thast reveres life, let alone one that claims to follow Jesus, entails a wholesale conversion of American culture away from the selfishness now dominating it. From the advertisers who shape our values to the teenagers who have been warped by noise and trashy entertainment, we have brought about a population upon whom the realities of the divine mystery make little impact. If we want health—from the prevention of abortion to the prevention of nuclear war, ecological ruin, and systemic poverty—we have to sacrifice our pretense that we Americans are little kings, able to abuse the world, other people, and our own bodies as we see fit.

Last, the women involved in decisions about conception, birth, and abortion have to sacrifice their version of the self-centeredness I have been pillorying. This, too, goes down hard in many feminist circles, for many bad reasons but also for a few good reasons. The good reasons, summarily, are that women have long been history's victims and should not be singled out for blame or special sacrifices today. These good reasons, of course, should factor in any specific decision about abortion. But women are not the only parties to decisions about the birth or termination of their fetuses, and in the name of realism they have to sacrifice the pretense that they are. I think there is a sense in which the woman carrying a child should have the primary say about that child's welfare, but I think that the attempt to make birth or abortion solely the mother's choice runs counter to the roles, and so the rights, of the father and society.

Even more importantly, however, it runs counter to the role and so the rights of the fetal child. This child is a human being, by all the criteria of prenatal biology and common sense. Its prenatal development of course runs a spectrum from potentiality to actuality, but the key reality is the final causality of the process: the birth of a new human being whom all tradition has considered as personal as its parents. Not to admit this causality, whether for philosophical reasons or because of biological theory, is to wander again into one of those self-chosen cul-de-sacs. We don't like the behavioral changes that acknowledging a given reality would imply so we deny that reality. It is the syndrome that Americans should know well from Vietnam, from their history of slavery, and from their treatment of women. It is the predominant pattern in our military dementia. Abroad it distorts socialist regimes that grossly abuse their citizens, from the Soviet Union to Cambodia, from Libya to Paraguay. Women carrying children know they have within them a being who relatively soon will be cooing, and then crawling, and then asking for help with its math. To pretend that this being is not human, has no rights, and should not be represented in abortion decisions is a dreadful fugue from reality. Once again, sacrificing this pretense would be a return to sanity.

· ADOPTION ·

Granted the foregoing considerations of prevention and sacrifice, we could have in place a policy that would greatly reduce the destruction of fetal life. However, only the hopelessly naive would think that even a thousandfold improvement in our attitudes and practices would eliminate unwanted pregnancies. For the vast majority of these pregnancies the solution which is most rational and consistent with the ethical viewpoint I have been developing is adoption. If the fetus is innocent humanity with the right to life, and if the woman carrying the fetus cannot expect to raise it well, then this woman, and the father of her child, and representatives of society at large ought to arrange for the child's being raised in other circumstances. At present we assume many of the arguments of the anti-abortion position and make adoption much more difficult than it should be.

I am not referring to the regulations that are designed to insure the child's welfare in an adoptive home. I am referring to the attitude that a child is only its parents' responsibility, and to the refinement of this attitude: the feeling that the pregnant woman got herself with child and that consequently the child is only her burden. One might be able to mount a defense of this position—I think it would be feeble—were there no appropriate people longing to adopt children. But in fact the mismatch between the huge number of fetuses being killed each year and the huge number of people wanting to adopt children is another sign of the dysfunction of our social systems. Just as the mismatch between the people going hungry in our society and the food being wasted shouts that we have an absurd system, so does the mismatch between abortion and the desire to adopt. The privacy of the adoption decision, as defined by the current law, once again flies in the face of the overall social reality and the overall common good.

Am I saying, then, that pregnant women who do not want to raise their child should be asked to carry it to term and give it over for adoption? Yes. As a general policy, with brackets for the moment placed around especially difficult cases, an ethics that honors the right of the fetus to life has to reach this conclusion if it is to be consistent. To take as an example the vast majority of pregnancies, in which the woman has played a willing or compliant role: both parents have the duty of honoring the rights of the life that they have generated, and so both parents should carry the process through to birth and adoption (if they cannot or will not raise the child themselves).

This said, I must move to some collateral considerations. First, society at large has to drop the moralism that surrounds sexuality and deal with it much more honestly, especially in the case of teenagers. The churches have to take to heart their own doctrinal conviction that sexual sins are less serious than sins of pride and destructive domination. There is no equivalence, for example, between an officer of a corporation that is systematically ripping off poor people at home and abroad and a young girl pregnant through a sexual misadventure. The former is at least potentially a sinner on the grand scale, truly a minion of Satan. The latter is a poor kid victimized by hormones, societal pressures, and the statistics of her cycle. We should not deal with her the way we deal with kids who skin their knees falling off their bikes, but we should deal with her rather matter-of-factly, providing her the financial and emotional support she needs to carry her child, stay at home, continue in school, and generally go on with as little disturbance of the positive parts of her normal routine as necessary.

Second, we have to confront the racial and ethnic dimensions of unwanted pregnancies honestly and mount attitudes toward adoption that encourage people to cross racial lines. This seems already to be happening, at least in small measure, and it is one of the most hopeful signs that we are starting to loosen the horrible hold that racism has had upon us. People who really want to lessen the number of abortions will labor as diligently for pregnant women outside the white mainstream as for the white middle classes. People who believe that killing fetal life is wrong and deranging will think that providing abortion on the demand of poor people from the societal margins is no genuine charity.

Third, and perhaps most controversial, we must consider changing our views of parenthood and child rearing sufficiently to allow married women who conceive an unwanted child to carry that child to term and then give it over for adoption. We would have to do this cautiously, of course, so as not to injure the usual bonds of parent-child affection and responsibility. We would have to protect poor people from pressures that would make them merely breeders for others. But a judicious development of such a policy would take away most of the rationale presently offered by married people who abort their fetuses because their family circumstances or personal needs make raising the child loom as impossibly onerous. No doubt many such people would continue to choose abortion, saying that even carrying the child to term would be an impossible burden. But this surely is a less telling argument than arguments based on the financial, psychological, and other demands that one can project raising a child from birth to age twenty-one would entail. The scheme can conjure up utopian scenarios, from that of Plato to that of George Orwell, which seem to consider child raising a function of society at large more than a function of the child's parents. I would not want to support such a view. I simply would want to make it socially acceptable for people who become pregnant inadvertently and against their design to find a decent way beyond the twin negative options of aborting the child or raising the child with traumatic results.

Most of what I have written about adoption thus far has had in mind the bulk of unwanted pregnancies which, either outside marriage or inside, have occurred through the partners' lack of care or bad luck. Generally we think that being adult and responsible means accepting the consequences of one's carelessness and bearing the common burden of living in a world that makes most of us unlucky from time to time. Moreover, we increase the pressure to perform in such an adult way in the measure that things of great moment are at stake. Thinking that few things are of more moment than human life, life which I attribute to the prenatal child, I find entirely defensible the requirement that the child's parents honor its right to exist by not aborting it.

But what about difficult cases such as rape or incest, in which the mother's free choice has been seriously curtailed or indeed completely absent? Further, what about cases in which prenatal examination gives nearly certain evidence that the child being carried is seriously defective? I would feel happier not passing judgment in these cases, because they demand significant scientific and ethical expertise, but rather than risk being charged with copping out or avoiding the actual situations in which thousands of people find themselves, I shall give them a try. First, I would be happiest if women pregnant through rape or incest could find it in themselves to dissociate the innocent child they are carrying from the horrible mode of its conception and so could carry the child to term. This seems to me the logic of seeing the child's right to exist as more important than a lesser right (existing well or less painfully) of its parents. Second, I would want the rapist or other partner to the incest to bear responsibility for his (usually it will be a male) role, especially in economic terms. Third, I would regret the choice of a woman raped or victimized by incest to abort, but if she could only hate the child or genuinely seemed to risk mental illness by carrying it I would accept her decision as what might be called a "justified unjustifiable" action. The legal aspects of such a case are better considered later, when we deal with politics. The moral aspects would seem to recall the situations in which people "have" to do things because of their psychic states—have to steal, kill, commit suicide, things they should not want to do, and probably do not want to do.

Fourth, I tentatively think that damaged fetuses that have overwhelming odds against their living outside the womb without extraordinary technological help can be destroyed (as painlessly as possible). The justification would be that in fact nature has curtailed their right to life or their realistic expectation of living. Fetuses that seem likely to survive but will be seriously defective mentally should be brought to term, and society should provide for them according to the degree of their deficiency. For example, mongoloid children (victims of Down's syndrome) who can live happy and useful lives should be placed in families, where this is possible. Fetuses likely to survive with no mental impairment but with strong physical impairments certainly should be preserved, since mentality and spirituality are even more central to humanity than is good physical health. Last, in cases where the life of the mother and the life of the child seem to conflict, I think it would be permissible to focus on saving the life of the mother and allowing the death of the prenatal child as an indirect and regretted side effect.

· BALANCE ·

Obviously, the more concrete and extensive one's examination of abortion, the more difficult it is to pass judgment. Many situations are terribly knotted. I have therefore preferred to concentrate on the attitudes that I think are central to both mental health and a vigorous Christian faith. The last of these is balance. I have anticipated it previously, in making the love of God and the variety of God's ways to "save" paramount. Evil as abortion is, it is not beyond the mercy of God, nor is it so singular an evil that we should become citizens or believers obsessed with it.

What we should be possessed with is a passion for life, in all of its gradations and overtones. The divine life of grace is the richest set of gradations and overtones, and this life spotlights love. The goodness of creation is the bedrock judgment, and this existential value ought always to serve us as a solid foundation—i.e., we ought to reverence all that is and make any proposal to destroy what is carry a strong burden of proof. This does not mean no discrimination between human beings and other creatures, nor does it mean no development of natural resources. It does mean that creation has rights independent of human beings and their legal systems. All the more so does it mean that all human beings have rights independent of the few human beings who fashion a society's lawt and control its economics and politics.

Between divine life at the top of the scale and creation as a solid foundation occur the lives and goods most often under consideration or even debate. All societies have to work out their choices and evaluations in this middle area, moving tentatively and prudentially. Societies can vary considerably in what they judge. For example, the place accorded the cow in Hindu society is not the place accorded the cow in ours, and Western ethicians have not been slow to criticize Hinduism for often seeming to prefer bovine life to human life. Still, the overall tendency has been for most societies to honor life more than good life, existence more than existence as wealthy, fully healthy, flourishing, etc. So, for example, the common view of murder has been that it is criminal and sinful: one person cannot take the life of another person merely to insure the first person's greater wealth, sexual satisfaction, or increase in political power. Similarly, Christian social teaching from the time of the church fathers has had the view that no one has the right to luxuries as long as anyone lacks necessities. In other words, the rights of starving people or people desperately in need of health care take priority over the desires of comfortable people to own bigger cars or eat more elegant meals. One can argue on the basis of this viewpoint that a large amount of our American expenditure for military development is unethical: As long as millions of people in our country lack necessities, or at least elementary goods, the upper reaches of national defense (esoteric technology), let alone the prosperity of the defense industries, must come second. (One can also argue, of course, that the defense enterprise, as currently conducted in a nuclear age, immorally endangers the primary right of most people to survival.)

At any rate, applied to the abortion controversy, considerations such as these seem to suggest the following balance of positions. First, the rights of the fetal child to existence should predominate over the rights of its parents to exist fully comfortably, and over the rights of society to keep its welfare budgets trim. Second, abortion occurs within a social field or cultural system, and only by shifting that whole field or system so that the divine mystery of love becomes primary would I expect the arguments against abortion, for adoption, and the like to become potent. Third, the religionists who make the private or personal choice of the mother the all-determining value are defending a good cause, but inordinately. The mother's right to exist well is important (more important than the father's right in this case, because of her closer connection with the child, and more important than society's rights), but it is less primordial and important than the right of the prenatal child to continue to be. Fourth, the feminism and secularism that motivate religious feminists to make "our right to choose" the motto and final touchstone should be respected for the forms of idealism and faith they carry, but they should also be exposed for the deficiencies they manifest. The this-worldly concerns of many people who reluctantly, yet in the final analysis really, come out in favor of abortion can be fine expressions of the sort of concern for the poor, and for a proper Christian incarnationalism, which motivated Jesus and fired the author of John's Gospel. Such people are rightly offended by the evils of poverty: ignorance, suffering, discrimination, ruined spirits as well as ruined bodies. In their case "existing well" is a quite defensible position. Moreover, they tend to champion downtrodden people who for too long have existed badly so that a few others could exist very well. Women historically and to the present day make up the majority of such people. Having read their Marx, such religious feminists want to avoid making religion an opiate that keeps an oppressive status quo going. Having read their biblical prophets, they want justice and the improvement of oppressed people's lives to roll down like a mighty stream. Calling such people liberation theologians is both accurate and deserves praise.

On the other hand, their advocacy of abortion suggests the limits or deficiencies in such religionists' faith, when one compares it to the (what I would consider) full-blown Christian entity. I can't picture Jesus aborting prenatal life, because I see Jesus living for a God who quite transcends time and its secular prospects. Jesus wanted people to live well, by the standards of the Kingdom, but he did not make living well the first of his values. Otherwise, he certainly would not have sacrificed himself on the cross so recklessly. We may properly ask what the best, most adequately demythologized translations of this biblical vision are, but in my opinion they will not turn out to justify killing prenatal children. I think that deep prayer, the sacrifice of worldly advantage, works of art or science done for the intrinsic good of understanding or making something beautiful, and honoring such immaterial yet quintessentially human realities as the rights of the vulnerable (including children, the most vulnerable of us all), are the main this-worldly or secular ways that Jesus' otherworldliness should be translated. Heaven, immortality, and resurrection, along with judgment and hell, are other ingredients that we have to factor in. A Christian secularism that would ignore either of these sets of translations is in my opinion inauthentic and not truly liberating. A Christian secularism that adequately takes them into account in my opinion will never come out pro-abortionist.[5]

·9·

POLITICS

· THE LIMITS OF LAW ·

We move from prudential theology to politics by reflecting on law. Law has a good aura, when one considers the disorders that reigned prior to the Magna Carta and other ground-breaking codifications of people's rights. Law has a bad aura, when one considers the inevitable gap between any codification and the living Spirit, or when one observes the ease with which law is manipulated as an instrument of oppression. One could say, for example, that both the codification and the administration of Soviet law give the common citizenry little real protection against its government. The large population of the Gulag Archipelago would be the most eloquent justification for this charge. Similarly, one could say that the history of law in the United States shows many serious twists of past tradition and present objectivity for the sake of continuing such oppressions as racism and sexism. The battles over slavery and women's suffrage are eloquent justifications of this charge.

The strength of John Noonan's work, *A Private Choice: Abortion in America in the Seventies,* my debt to which I have already acknowledged, is its analysis of both the content and the surrounding atmosphere of the abortion law created by the Supreme Court's decision in *Roe* v. *Wade* in 1973. I would agree with critics of Noonan, such as Beverly Harrison, that the pregnant woman who inevitably is the reference of much of Noonan's discussion seems wrongly depersonalized by such terminology as "the carrier" or "the gravida." On the stark implications of the abortion law itself, however, I find Noonan's work very important. Whether or not one

126

agrees with either his assumptions or his arguments, he relentlessly presses the key issue upon the reader: abortion is the killing of innocent prenatal human life. Nor has Noonan, himself a professor of law at the University of California at Berkeley, been alone in his thorough-going criticism of the 1973 Court and the writer of the majority decision, Justice Harry Blackmun. Among contemporary constitutional lawyers he can cite the cream of the crop as harshly critical of the new law: Archibald Cox, Alexander Bickel, Richard Epstein, Harry Wellington, and John Hart Ely. Among illustrious predecessors, true pillars of the theoretical foundations of American Constitutional law, he can invoke Justices Holmes, Brandeis, and Frankfurter. At the least, then, Noonan makes a plausible case that *Roe* v. *Wade* was bad law.[1]

The limits of the law probably strike the Christian theologian in a distinctive fashion. The polemics of the apostle Paul against the Jewish law have been so influential in Christian theology, especially that of Protestantism, that the limits of human law easily become a symbol of human impotence and sin. Recent scholarship has somewhat rehabilitated the Jewish Torah, and somewhat mitigated Paul's critique of it. It remains true, however, that Christian theology will never validly put law of any sort over individual conscience, let alone over the Holy Spirit. From Peter saying, "We must obey God rather than men" (Acts 5:29), to the ultimately more crucial example of Jesus being put to death quite legally, through the collusion of both Jews and Romans who professed to be acting within their peoples' codes, Christians have ready to hand a potent fund of lessons in the limits of human law. If they know their own faith they will always place freedom and justice outside the law, in the grace of God. If they know their own church's history and do not edit out such chapters as the Inquisition, they will realize that canon law is as liable to human distortion as any other human codification. So the ancient wisdom that one should not place one's trust in princes definitely extends to the princes', or the people's, law. We have "here" no lasting city, and we have in temporal law no sure repository of justice.

This said, one has of course to say such further things as the need for law, the obligation of citizens to follow the law wherever possible, and the sometimes heroic service that judges and attorneys provide in trying to make the law a means of justice. The limits of the law finally are but the limits of ourselves as sinful, self-serving creatures. Lao Tzu observed long ago that in the mythic early age, when people lived close to nature and in fuller human vigor, there were virtually no laws and no criminals. The law and criminality arose together, and their coexistence has always been mutually stimulating. Paul had something of the same intuition. Law makes people aware of their moral failures but does not lead to repentance. When law comes to dominate the cultural horizon, as one can make a good case for saying it does today, moral sensitivity can shrink to the "legal," meaning by that: "what we can slip through the cracks in the codes."

A judgment about the morality of abortion, therefore, is almost bound to be trivial if it limits itself to what the 1973 law allowed and overtly expressed. Judges, of course, have to limit the bases of their decisions to legal parameters, but theologians, reflecting on the sort of life that a people's laws and all their other cultural tools ought to be developing, are not so limited. Theologians, moralists, and legal thinkers (when they look to the foundations and goals of their discipline), have to consider politics not just as the art of what is possible in the strict sense of the present codes but also as the art of leading out the best of a people's traditions and present instincts. In this latter consideration, politics is inseparable from education, as we shall more fully reflect in the final section of this chapter.

What, then, are the most relevant and general considerations that should structure a faith-filled reflection on the current American politics of abortion? Perhaps first, that it is as impure as all the other areas of American political life. The debates over abortion have economic, philosophical, and "political" (in the sense of garnering votes) engines, just as the debate about the military budget and foreign policy stances toward Latin American countries do. People jump into these debates, lobby, apply pressure on legislators for as many ideological reasons as they do when the issue is building nuclear weapons or funding the Nicaraguan Contras. The only peculiarity of the abortion debate, in the opinion of those who believe that fetal life is human and personal, is the simplicity of the moral bottom line. For these people—who are no small fraction of the American citizenry, indeed, they may be the majority, depending on how a pollster frames the relevant questions—the fetus is both innocent and possessed of fundamental rights equal to those of its parents or any other members of society at large. Even passionate advocates of nuclear disarmament cannot claim that the Soviets or our other potential military adversaries are so innocent.

Presently one of the limits to the American law on abortion, and so of the American political struggle over the issue, is the way that ideology has made clear perception difficult. Feminists and others concerned to safeguard the rights and minister to the needs of women suffering unwanted pregnancies charge that anti-abortionists are acting out a longstanding sexism and show no compassionate understanding of a uniquely female sort of suffering. They often claim, as well, that opposition to abortion on demand penalizes the poor and so is laden with racism and economic injustice. Opponents of abortion, for their part, claim that pro-abortionists are pagans in revolt from God and from the most elementary realities of traditional Western morality: you don't kill your young. They further charge, as I have, that the blindness to the rights of prenatal children revealed in abortion is part and parcel of a general cultural sickness brought about by the victories of mammon and material self-centeredness. To put this charge differently: Who would be surprised to find the yuppie readers of *Time* or *New York Magazine* in favor of abortion?

· MAJORITY RIGHTS ·

A democracy is supposed to move by the will of the people. As a political form, it assumes that governments derive their right to rule from the consent of the governed. One of the most central criticisms of the 1973 abortion law was that it seemed to be taking the judiciary beyond its proper role and usurping the right of the legislative branch to enact new laws and express the will of the people. The judiciary, not being directly elected by the people, should not be the forum for interpreting the people's will and attempting to express that will to regulative effect. The executive branch of the American government can claim to be expressing the will of the people, as can the regulations developed by the agencies that the elected executives control, but they can rightly do this only in dialectical relation to the legislative branch. This principle of checks and balances therefore derives much of its plausibility from the judgment that the three branches of democratic government will both serve the will of the people and keep that will from being thwarted, from being simplistically interpreted, or from being made the thoughtless demands of a lusty mob.

In a society that preaches the equal creation of all human beings and the divine endowment of all with alienable rights, leading and serving public opinion become delicate tasks. As long as the people have confidence in their elected officials and in the appointed officials these elected officials choose, government can bump along in relatively good shape. When great matters such as war, economic policy, and care of the elderly cause widespread division, the common people have to be brought to express their will more vigorously. In the historic cases of slavery and women's suffrage, this process set sibling against sibling. Those on the side that history came to call losing could cite high-mindedness: Washington and Jefferson could be numbered among the slavers. Those on the side that history came to call winning could often claim both high-mindedness and a majority of the popular support: even if Lincoln had found himself expressing a minority view of the need for emancipation, he could cite "higher" laws and dictates of conscience for his position. "Majority" rule is therefore hardly a simple matter. This seems completely true in the case of abortion. What the polls say is hardly the final word.

Nonetheless, a government truly wanting to exist of, by, and for the people would take pains to determine what the citizenry thinks about a matter of such moral significance as abortion. As in the case of a decision to go to war, one could not necessarily wait for the results of a mass mailing of ballots, but one could put aside party advantage and make a special effort to discern what the popular morality seemed to be. For the conscientious politician the results could never be determinative—we all retain the final responsibility to judge what we think is right and wrong, and to act in accord with this judgment—but they could be highly instructive. One would hope, for example, that politicians who found themselves seriously at odds with their constituencies would reconsider the propriety of their public service.

The politicians one now sees on the national scene do not seem to act in this straightforward manner (determine as best I can where the people I represent stand, and then determine whether I can conscientiously advance their majority opinion). They waffle and double-speak and invoke compromise as the fundamental law of political life. Some of this, of course, makes good sense. A pluralistic and democratic society does have to move by way of compromise. But some of it is highly suspect or even patently dishonest. In the measure that one is dealing with life and death issues, compromise of this latter sort will not do.

It is hard to pass final judgment on the celebrated dilemma of Catholic politicians such as Geraldine Ferraro and Mario Cuomo, whose attempt to find a via media between what they themselves judge about the morality of abortion and what they will support as elected officials has received perhaps improperly extensive coverage by agents of the news media who want to make concern about abortion a purely Catholic idiosyncracy. After some reflection, however, I have tentatively decided that their middle ground is inadequate. I don't see in the case of these two officials the straightforward procedure of polling one's constituency, clarifying one's own conscience, and judging one's aptness for political office in terms of the match or mismatch between the two. My sense is that neither politician was courageous enough to seek the actual facts of public opinion, confront the clashes with the present law of the land that this opinion might portend, sharpen his or her own moral judgment about abortion (which certainly could go against the verdict of the polls), and then take a clean stand about the politics to be pursued: either the full elaboration of the abortion liberty that a positive personal judgment on the morality of abortion would imply, or the full effort to obtain the repeal of the abortion liberty that a sharp negative judgment on the morality of abortion would imply.

But is this way of phrasing things not an invitation to single issue politics, with its attendant monomania? Certainly this way of shading things runs that risk, but it need not reach that conclusion. A Geraldine Ferraro could rightly say that her overall suitability for office depends on much more than her position on abortion. She could then lay out her position on other issues of great significance and let her constituency judge how suitable they found this overall profile. I think she would have been better off, even politically, to have followed through on the consequences of her professed personal opposition to abortion and pledged herself to work for the repeal of the current law and the radical diminution of actual abortions. I think that would have been more honest, consistent, and decisive. By wandering into distinctions between what she would do privately and how she would vote and lobby in her public capacity she introduced a confusion that merely added more mud to already polluted political waters.

Across the land, we suffer from a dearth of politicians who are properly simple in presenting their ethical position. Across the land, staying in office (or gaining office) often seems to mean more than staying faithful to one's moral personhood. Abortion has dramatized the revelations of this gross deficiency among our national leaders. Because it is volatile as few other issues, it is hedged, fudged, and compromised as few other issues. To be sure, this judgment probably condemns as many anti-abortion politicos as it does those who favor the abortion liberty. A politician such as Ronald Reagan, who is on record as fully opposed to abortion,[2] must raise doubts about the sincerity of his commitment when his defense and economic policies seem to favor death or mammon rather than life or the poor. Conversely, many of the representatives most eloquent and consistent in defending the rights of the poor and the cause of peace fall on the side of favoring the abortion liberty. They keep the plight of women pregnant with unwanted children paramount, block out the existence and rights of the prenatal human being, and so make abortion a matter of humanitarian liberalism. Only a few politicians seem consistently to discern and support the seamless garment of ethical commitment to life and justice. Only a few seem to fashion their positions in terms of basic physical realities and moral imperatives, rather than in terms of staying in office. The peculiarity of the abortion issue is that the apparent, and to my mind healthy, will of the majority of the electorate should have been thwarted so long and so thoroughly. Even when a clear majority in the House of Representatives wanted to restrict the abortion liberty through the Hyde amendment, the Senate and such branches of the executive as the Department of Health and Human Services, along with the federal judiciary, maneuvered to thwart this will. The majority of our public servants did not want to acknowledge the will of the majority on abortion, because they did not want to serve it. The majority of our public servants did not number prenatal children among their constituency, because they did not want to face how their actions were supporting the widespread killing of this part of the democratic population.

· MINORITY RIGHTS ·

In a democracy, the views and rights of the majority should usually prevail. If officials find themselves at odds with these views, whether through failing to win reelection on the basis of their frank promulgation of their personal stands or through polling that they consider reliable, they should judge the times unfit for their public service. They continue to have channels through which they might convert the majority of public opinion to their position, of course. The theoreticians of democratic government soon saw that government by the people depends on freedom of information and speech. The persuasion that Plato found an ingredient in effective political rule remains the key component in democratic societies, even when we find it as tangled as the other morally impure aspects of such societies. The sine qua non without which democratic societies cannot function even tolerably well is honest expression of opinion and honest debate. Both of these will be geared more to clarifying the truth than to winning election, gaining economic advantage, securing more political power, and other lesser goods (or even evils).

The smokescreen that the defenders of the abortion liberty have created around what is probably their minority position is a telling index of the impurity of their motivation. By perverting language and stacking committees, they have connived to write the prenatal human being out of existence. This accomplished, they think they can speak of abortion as a "procedure" equal to birth in terminating pregnancy. They have further connived to block out the participation and interests of the fetus in abortion procedures, and to refer to what obviously is a human child as simply "the products of conception." Consequently, it is easy for them to dismiss the effects of abortion as "wastage," and to imply that child and placenta stand on the same level. The right of the minority to undergo an action of highly dubious morality, like the right of the medical agent to perform such an action, has become sacrosanct. This turns traditional Judaeo-Christian ethics on its head, praising an action that was traditionally condemned. It also makes the right of the few to kill prevail over the right of the many to either survive or have their abhorrence of prenatal killing honored.

At the least, the rights of the minority to benefit from public policies should not countervail the rights of the majority. Specifically, a majority opposed to a liberty should not be taxed so that a minority can enjoy it. Anti-abortionists would still have an imperative agenda were the government not in the business of funding abortions, but their agenda is doubly crowded when they reflect that they are being forced to pay for what they regard as heinous sin. It would be quite similar to being taxed for the waging of a war judged thoroughly immoral. In Christian tradition, if not American political tradition, the rights of the conscientious objector have a high standing. Those whose consciences strenuously object to abortion, the public funding of abortions, and the government's efforts to spread the abortion liberty as an alternative to expensive welfare payments should put heavy pressure on their representatives to overthrow this wagging of the dog by the tail. They should resist if need be by nonviolent civil disobedience—the now hallowed means of expressing conscientious objection—efforts to force hospitals and medical personnel to become agents of an abortion law and government medical policy that they abhor on moral grounds. With theologians and ethicians, they should labor to make the philosophical position of the minority stand forth in all its eccentricity and godlessness. Without becoming politically monomaniacal, they should clarify the implications of an ethics consistently in favor of life and urge those to whom this links them in matters of military and economic policy to see the logical connections to matters of policy on abortion (in effect telling pacifists and those on the side of the poor that they are terribly illogical to sponsor the killing of prenatal children).

What, then, about the rights of those people who feel in conscience that they not only may abort prenatal human life but in a given situation actually should abort it (for the sake of the overall welfare of their family, or for the sake of their psychic survival, or for some other good they think greater than the existence of the fetus that is soon to be an independently existing human being)? Doesn't a candidate for national office such as Geraldine Ferraro, and an ethician concerned with the prosperity of the entire population of a democracy, have to bend over backwards to protect the God-given and Constitution-given rights of people in minority positions?

They do indeed, and figuring out how to execute this responsibility without harming the even greater rights of the majority is perhaps the most difficult task that ethics imposes on those working in a pluralistic democracy. In this matter of abortion, several judgments come to mind which may clarify how the decision ought to eventuate. First, there is the apt observation that on the whole the 1973 abortion law does not compel any woman to have an abortion. With possible qualification when it comes to the participation of taxpayers at large and medical personnel, the law allows abortion rather than commanding it. Thus people who have no desire to commit or undergo abortion do not have to do so. One might argue that the effects of the law are therefore parallel to the effects of the laws on freedom of speech in the area of pornography: just as no one is forced to buy, read, or view pornographic materials, so no one is forced to hie off to an abortion clinic and undergo the procedure. The analogy obviously limps, however, in that in the case of abortion the prenatal child whose destruction is involved begs serious consideration. In other words, there is a party to any abortion that may well not want to participate (common sense would dictate that one representing the prenatal child would have to advance its rights to exist). Abortion forces it to participate and be destroyed.

Second, there is the recourse that all minority groups have to the mechanisms by which public opinion and law are changed in a democracy. The pro-abortionists in fact used these mechanisms brilliantly to engineer the liberty provided by the 1973 decision and then to broaden its implications. The anti-abortionists should not be charged with anything more than an equally astute use of the democratic process, should they succeed in overthrowing that liberty (for example, by achieving a Constitutional amendment that would ban abortions or public funding of abortions). Third, one might distinguish between allowing abortions, ideally in very restricted circumstances, and funding them from public funds. One might also distinguish between restricting women's access to abortions and bringing criminal charges against women for having abortions. One could also distinguish the penalties to be leveled against those who perform the abortions and against the women who undergo abortions as patients. In other words, a wide range of legal options is possible. Abortion law that permitted procedures only during the first trimester would be preferable to the current law which is not as restrictive. Abortion law that limited procedures to cases of rape and incest would be preferable to wider interpretation of the liberty. Positive law that required counseling in contraceptive techniques acceptable to the mother's conscience (yes, there are women who would not scruple to abort but would scruple to use artificial contraceptives, weird as that may sound) could be a great boon. The limits of good law significantly are the limits of good legal imagination. The proper rights of the minority need not be completely washed away by a repeal of the current legal interpretation and governmental policies prosecuted as the will of the majority.

· EDUCATION ·

I shall be foolish enough to conclude this section with a sketch of the legal and political situation that I think anti-abortionists ought to target, or really an educational effort I would have them mount. But first let me recall the perspective of faith that determines my convictions. Concluding an article on what light the New Testament sheds on peacemaking, Sandra M. Schneiders has written an eloquent paragraph which I find germane to the analogous fight for the lives of the unborn:

> Yet the basic issue is not whether this [policy of not using nuclear weapons in any situation] is a reasonable strategy. The Gospel's peacemaking mandate, its love command, the ministry of reconciliation which it entrusts to the Christian community, the preferential option for the poor to which it calls us, and the reversal dynamic inaugurated by the resurrection of Jesus which it proclaims are not just the requirements of human nature or the conclusions of enlightened rationality. They are a new wine which must burst the wineskins of the ancient dynamics of competition and conflict, aggression and hatred, retaliation, the oppression of the poor and the weak by the rich and the powerful, and the search for unlimited human security and national supremacy upon which our current defense policy is based. In other words, the Gospel's contribution to our reflection on war and peace is neither accidental nor purely exhortatory. It is substantive and structural. The question is whether the dynamics of Christian discipleship are reconcilable with the dynamics of national policy in the area of defense. If the answer is no, then those who call themselves Christians have hard choices to make. One of the most encouraging signs of the maturity and commitment of Christians in our time is that

increasing numbers of Christians are making those choices and
making it clear that the source of their convictions and their
actions is the Gospel they profess.[3]

I would want the source of any Christian's convictions and actions
concerning abortion to be the Gospel that he or she professes.
Whether Denise Lardner Carmody, Geraldine Ferraro, Mario
Cuomo, or anyone else, a Christian who did not take to heart and
make structural Christ's good news to the poor, Christ's resurrection into new life, would be a very incomplete believer. Do the
dynamics of Christian discipleship allow the promotion of the liberty
to abort prenatal human life? Is the killing of unborn children recon-
cilable with the preaching, death, resurrection, and sending of the
Spirit of Jesus Christ? In my view, the answer to both questions
clearly is no. In my view, any advocacy of abortion on Christian
grounds, whether the supposed non-personhood of the fetus or the
priority of the needs or conscience of the pregnant woman, doesn't
fly. I think that Jesus' whole posture makes him a passionate advocate of the life of the most vulnerable, and that Jesus certainly would
number prenatal children among them. Finally, I don't think that
the changes that have occurred since Jesus' time, either the growth
in world population or the development of women's rights, invali-
date these judgments. The judgments rest on more basic and ultimate grounds or choices: life or death, nurturing and protecting or
killing.

Consequently, I think that Catholic Christian anti-abortionists
should mount a civil but strong educational campaign, as perhaps
their episcopal leaders now think they are doing or plan to do in the
future, that would stress the changes in both mentality and legal
structure necessary to prevent abortions from taking place. The
first focus of such a campaign would be the sex education and contraception mentioned above when we considered prevention in the
context of prudential theology. The second focus would be the facili-
tation of adoption that we also considered. The third focus would be
a movement to change the present legal structure and policies of
governmental agencies so as to shut down the abortion industry. I
think that abortion probably has to be categorized as illegal if the
moral prohibitions against it raised by the status of the prenatal
human being are to be effective. I would wish that moral impera-

tives were enough, but the general behavior of the population at large suggest they are not. I would attach criminal sanctions to performing abortions, but I would not make having one a criminal act. (I think the majority of women have abortions reluctantly, and that criminalizing their actions only punishes victims further. No doubt there are cases in which mothers carrying children do have a truly murderous intent, but I would tolerate those as marginal.) I have not decided about cases of rape and incest, beyond what I mentioned previously, so I would ask the counsel of people more learned in psychiatry and the law than I about the likely part of wisdom in such cases. My legal suggestions in the cases where the life of the mother is endangered by childbirth, or where the prenatal child has been diagnosed as seriously defective, would allow the latitude I suggested previously.

To make this sort of legislation rational if not accepted in all quarters, one would have to make very persuasive the fully human status of the prenatal child and the reasons for according it the rights of a person. I think the most salient factors in this regard come from human embryology and the study of prenatal processes. They show that from sixty days the child, no bigger than a human thumb, has most of its critical organs in place. They make it clear that from fertilization a process gets under way which ineluctably intends the development of another member of our human species. We can only shield ourselves from this reality by perverting or ignoring the bare facts of the process. We can only shield ourselves, I think, by preferring the liberty to abort to what reality and conscience say is so. Traditionally we have better honored reality and conscience and have been better able to endow silent, vulnerable beings such as prenatal children with their proper moral and legal rights. The education that we need to return our culture to spiritual health will therefore target the materialism and self-centeredness that have weakened our capacity for judging honestly and acting bravely.

One final educational matter, which will no doubt come into play more fully in the next chapter, is the relative priorities that my point of view assigns to feminism and Christianity. I would hope that the first half of this book has established the depth of my judgment that feminism, in the sense of advancing women's full equality in humanity with men, is a moral imperative. I have had to work through considerable amounts of feminist theory to reach this judgment of the

second half of the book that the rights of women to kill their prenatal children are less significant than the rights of those children,
at least half of whom would be the prime subjects of feminist care
in the next generation, to exist. In fact, I have had to accept the
judgment of the anti-abortionists that "killing" is the proper and
realistic term to use. "The termination of pregnancy," I have come
to agree, badly obscures the actual realities of what goes on in abortion clinics. One should speak accurately and without blocking out
the gross physical realities of the acts one is performing or sanction-
ing. Physicians and psychologists who have been converted from an
advocacy of abortion to an abjuration of abortion generally have
been greatly moved by observing and reflecting on what actually
occurs in the process of an abortion. The tiny human being lying in
the bloody bucket or scattered as bits of mashed flesh has, often
despite their best efforts to discount it, forced the light of conscience
still shining in them to confess it to be human, a child like their own
children, a terribly abused victim.

·10·

CONCLUSION

· CATHOLIC RADICALISM ·

We have now looked at the two crosses that I suggested might provide us a fine double entry into Catholic feminism. Ordination allowed us to consider the failings of Catholic Christianity with regard to women. Abortion allowed us to see the heart of darkness threatening feminism. Unequal as these two moral burdens may be, they both thrust the Catholic Christian feminist toward deeper ground. Only the God always greater than institutions and ideologies can ground a truly liberating spirituality. How might this conviction, so well expressed through Protestant Christian annals, gain a voice distinctively Catholic and feminist? My instinct is that by reflecting on Jesus' own twofold commandment with special sensitivity to the sacramental and feminist overtones it bears today we may catch the timbre we seek.

First, the love of God, filial and sororal, that Jesus conjures up immediately places one outside the clutches of institutions and ideologies. As noted by reference to Muslim terrorists, our other-worldly loves do have to be sane, and no doubt the best ballast for such sanity is truly seeing other people and other creatures—truly seeing this world—as objectively valuable in God's sight. But for the moment I mainly want to argue the case (exposed in full historical sweep by Eric Voegelin in his marvelous *Order and History*[1]) that proper order only comes to the human spirit when that spirit follows its most central hunger to a transcendent source of nourishment. The Johannine imagery of the bread and water of everlasting life is entirely germane here. That the most incarnational of the gospels, the

140

one in which the eschatology is most realized or this-worldly, should constantly situate Jesus' deepest identity in his relationship to his eternal Father, and should constantly explain the salvation available through faith in Jesus by the otherworldly source, calls all with ears to hear to a Christian version of the Muslim cry of faith: There is no God but the God revealed by Jesus Christ, and there is no human order except through acknowledging this God.

The totality or holism demanded by the first of Jesus' two commands of love echoes the Old Testament. It suggests a term that we usually encounter now in the context of Nazism, but which originally had a much more positive connotation: holocaust. The entirety of the offering that the believer was to make to God could be symbolized by burning the sacrificial victim completely. The whole mind, heart, soul, and strength of which Jesus speaks is the only measure appropriate to the divine immensity. And as is true of Islam, the immediate consequence of this holism is an abhorrence of idolatry. To set anything less than God in the shrine of the heart is utterly to pervert the human personality. This remains true when idolatry becomes more sophisticated, substituting financial security or sexual freedom or human autonomy for the force of the storm or the fertility of the god of the harvest.

A Catholic Christianity feminist spirituality after my heart will therefore be radically religious. Today one might best express this by saying that it will be fully absorbed with the mystery as which God tends to appear to us today. The depth and entirety, the height and the silence—all of our figures for what is most basic and haunting about existence, as human consciousness encounters its primordiality and promise, figure in the spirituality we need to be most realistic. Whenever we define "realism" in unmysterious, purely positivistic or empirical terms, we woefully denature ourselves. A feminist spirituality accepting this religious truism will find itself either cast out of many sisterhoods or forced to parse out difficult declensions of "spirituality," to find whether in fact they intuit and serve a genuinely transcendent divinity. The Catholic polish to this religiosity is the instinct to find the mystery close, near, full of grace, quickly involved with material creation and so productive of sacraments. The mystery confessed to be primordial and the sole source of true personal order is not far above us and beyond our reach. It is here, now, coming to us through words and deeds, people and plants, all the sights and sounds and flesh and blood that confect our humanity. Jesus, the incarnate Word, insures that this will be so. Children, born and prenatal, prompt such a faith, taking our breath away in hope and love.

That we should also love our neighbors as ourselves is the command of Jesus that returns us to sisterhoods and brotherhoods healthy and joyous out of commitment to make this world a place fit to live in. For our present purposes the passionate love of a mother for her small closest neighbors may be the most apposite:

> She looked at the clock. It was two-thirty; soon the children would be home. She waited for the sound of their arrival as if she were dressed for a party, listening for a taxi. No one had told her what it would be like, the way she loved her children. What a thing of the body it was, as physically rooted as sexual desire, but without its edge of danger. The urge to touch one's child, she often thought, was like, and wasn't like, the hunger that one felt to touch a lover: it lacked the suspense and greed and the component parts of insecurity and vanity that made so trying the beloved's near approach. Once the children were in the house, the air became more vivid and more heated: every object in the house grew more alive. How I love you, she always wanted to say, and you can never know it. I would die for you without a thought. You have given to my life its sheerest, its profoundest pleasure. But she could never say that. Instead, she would say, "How was school?" "Was lunch all right?" "Did you have your math test?"[2]

The passion of this quotation, with its nearly comic bit of concluding balance, suggests the immediacy of the sort of Catholic feminism I would love to see unfold. Because of its honor for the love that moves the stars, its obedience to the first part of Jesus' commandment, it could clasp children and other bits of life, warmth, beauty, and vulnerability to its bosom in an exultation that never lost humor and realism. This is the way we ourselves want to be loved: in all of our immediacy and humorous imperfection. This is the love that resurrects human suffering and makes the final play comedy rather than tragedy. And for me this is the love that imports the unfathomable roots of a life of faith. The person centered in such a love, gambling on such a love, clinging to Jesus as the icon of such a love is very different indeed from the person who doesn't know or honor it. Though they share the same mysterious border to all of their consciousness and significance, and though they experience many of the same sorts of stimuli to sorrow and joy, the sister who believes will always be a conundrum to the sister who does not believe, and vice-versa. The sister who believes, going to the roots of the Catholic sacramental interpretation of grace and human experience, will find many of the unbelieving sister's judgments and choices strangely flat or excessive or shy of the beauty they might have. Often the unbelieving sister will seem discontented beyond measure, as though she had forgotten the limits to all created achievements and knew little of the grace that intimates fulfillments the human heart can barely conceive.

For her part, the unbelieving sister may well find the believer irrationally sanguine or free of anger or measured in appetite. Indeed, the unbeliever may find the believer no fully trustworthy sister, rightly suspecting that the this-worldly movement of feminism can never contain her or command her full allegiance. The two types that I have sketched, to be sure, seldom exist full-blown. Not only are many purportedly religious sisters unauthentic; many purportedly secular or irreligious sisters love the mystery of life and creativity passionately. As well, many spend themselves to the utmost for their neighbors. The question then is simply which system of ideas better renders the actual dynamics of human growth in light and love. I'm quite willing to speak up for a radically Catholic Christian feminism, on the grounds that it is a superb exegesis of those reasons of the heart that most secular minds don't know or honor very well.

· LADY WISDOM ·

In Rosemary Haughton's superb work, *The Passionate God*,[3] the reasons of the divine heart emerge as a credible wisdom of love and evolution. From our human side, the wisdom to appreciate the divine strategy of exchange, with its breakthroughs and ravishments, appears just as the Hebrew Bible intuited, as a lovely feminine persona able to move gracefully to the divine measures. This sort of grace which renders the divine life sacramental is of course not limited to a Catholic feminist spirituality. The aesthetic forms that

Zen Buddhism has generated, for example, from the tea ceremony to swordsmanship and floral arrangement, brim with the infusions of Prajnaparamita, the Lady Wisdom who has gone beyond all this-worldly, karmic containments. Nonetheless, it is especially congenial to the Catholic instinct for incarnationalism and the Catholic hopefulness about human nature. Perhaps meditating on such a sapiential profile in the context of ordination and abortion will help us gain a more secure hold on it.

Concerning ordination, the Lady Wisdom would seem to suggest that ministerial service and liturgical leadership both ought to be beautiful and gracious. To be sure, their beauty and grace will not be that of the League of Women Voters or the Junior League. Good as the political and charitable works of those two organizations can be, they always seem in danger of averting their faces from the depths of ugliness and sin that spawn the problems they would ameliorate. I hold no brief for the position that women are less realistic about evil than men, since I find marginalized people the best experts in suffering. But I have found women colluding with the strategies of avoidance or shielding that ease the way of the great evil-doers of our time, whether abortionists or executives of the asbestos industry.[4] The women who complain that the chef at the club puts the chile relleño into bell peppers instead of green peppers don't want to live realistically. Instead of urinating they tinkle. Instead of facing the systemic evils that twist the lives of so many in their town they complain about the laziness of the help. Lady Wisdom moves to a power and beauty they don't want to fathom. Life on the surface is all too comfortable if hardly fulfilling, and they haven't got the guts to risk chucking it. A priesthood of women committed to the Crucified Lord could greatly benefit them. If they were communing at the hands of women no less sensitive than they but markedly stronger and more realistic, they might drop some of their shields and accept responsibility for some of the suffering atop which they sit.

This sort of reflection applies in spades to abortion. The Lady Wisdom who played before God at creation and so often figures in a maternal divine love changes in my mind's eye to Kali, the fierce destroyer, when confronted with great affronts to life like abortion. The more sharply we draw her in lines of compassion and understanding for life's most vulnerable creatures, the more fiercely we have to picture her condemnation of what attacks and kills life's most vulnerable creatures. The Lady can be at least as sophisticated as we, of course, and so can also extend compassion to women brought to the pass of abortion. She can understand the thread of good intention that runs through the bloody tapestry, even though she must call such a solution to a woman's sorry plight stupid and destructive. Were she to be represented by a corps of well-educated women priests, we might have a more effective ministry to unwed mothers, victims of abortion, and the powers who must be converted if abortion, and cognate disregard of the sanctity of life, is ever to diminish.

What is the access to Lady Wisdom that can keep Christian feminists fierce in their opposition to evil yet more filled with the love of Christ? My best suggestion is a contemplative prayer that moves between the divine no-thingness and daily life, in all of its tragedy and comedy, to their mutual illumination. The wisdom to see things in ultimate perspective under the aspect of eternity is of course a gift of the Holy Spirit. To have the lovely balance symbolized by the Lady is a more than human achievement. Yet there are human means applauded by all the saints who have achieved this balance, and paramount among them is regular prayer. Unless we drop out of the daily bustle on a regular basis, greeting the source of all our moral light in the quiet of early morning and tallying up our accounts by the quiet of the late night, we will be swept away. Without the anchor that only the otherness, the no-thingness, the silent mystery of the Creator affords, we will think we have here a lasting city. Then we will be sorely tempted to put our trust in princes and princesses of time, only to have them let us down again and again. Unless we are completely stupid, this let-down will bring us into crisis, forcing us to face the absurdity that humanity on its own ever strews. To be sure, such a crisis may be the beginning of a conversion to the truly mysterious and trans-human God. But that is not the inevitable result, however much we should trust that the grace of God often brings it about. There are too many cynics and burnt out cases about, cluttering up the offices of liberation and botching up its works, for one who sees clearly to be sure all is well. That would be like assuming that any alcoholic is sure to hit bottom and rebound into sober health. The grace of God does embrace everything, even the most squalid alleys of the Bowery and the most acidified cynic's soul. The Lady Wisdom nonetheless says that a great deal of human disorder and suffering should not be so. Sin, she says, is culpable irrationality, hurtful to more than just the sinner herself. As the sufferings of the alcoholic's family lie on the alcoholic's conscience, a huge lump of distress that the God who alone measures final responsibilities must assess, so the disedification and discouragement that ripple out from those who are defeated by excessive this-worldliness lie on their uncontemplative spirits.

It is not true, however, that contemplation of the divine mystery makes one a complete alien. Before enlightenment, trees are trees and stones are stones. In the middle of the conversion process, when one is rejecting the flat facticity of secularism as deadly to the human spirit, trees and stones overturn, begging their meaning and reason to be from something non-contingent. At the end of the conversion process, however, when one is mature in spirituality (though hardly perfect and still needing deeper conversion), trees are again trees and stones are again stones, yet all is different. The difference is that now trees, stones, and all other creatures bear a much more potent sacramentality. The materiality that previously made them heavy, closed to the spirit that can only operate at the upper reaches (say, where computer information lodges), now is rounded out, pregnant with intimations of grace. Flatland has become a land of liturgical richness: speech on the verge of poetry, movements on the verge of ballet. Bread and wine continue to be simple means of nourishment, but now very densely, compacting a great richness of symbolic suggestion. Flesh and blood continue to be fully finite, yet now they just might bear an only-begotten Son. And the people of God, from bums to barons, just might be the Body of Christ, bruised by sin yet ever irradiated by grace. The mystery, then, is greatly humanized. The God who truly is no thing moves through space and time. One cannot say what this God is, apart from pointing to the paradigm of Jesus (or lesser prophets). One can say, with great conviction, that this God is, because one has experienced, day in and day out, that "humanity" is correlative to "mystery." We are the creatures who live, move, and have our conscious being in a more, a plenum, that we shall never exhaust. We are the creatures who need only pray to find the wilderness reconfiguring itself and a path standing clear.

· AUTHENTICITY ·

Another way of picturing the path that can lead us through the wilderness of contemporary ethical confusion, tutoring our instincts about such painful phenomena as Catholic Christianity's refusal of ordination to women and secular feminism's readiness to support the liberty of abortion, is as the light that we cast in front of us when we decide conscientiously. My bias in this matter, as I have already indicated, is the analysis of consciousness developed by transcendental Catholic theologians such as Bernard Lonergan and Karl Rahner. Lonergan's analysis allows one to equate the maturation of a Christian conscience with following the light of judgment and the unrestricted love that the deeper dimensions of decision call forth. Rahner's analysis allows one to call the mystery that our examination of conscience tends to heighten the gracious God who has made the divine self-offer present everywhere. Both theologians provide a solid basis for dialogue with any person of good will, since both tie the key Christian existentials of sin and grace to the experiences that all human beings have of heeding or disobeying the call of conscience.

Let us examine ordination and abortion in this light. What does the call to authenticity or fidelity to conscience imply for these two issues that afflict Catholic feminism? First, in the case of ordination, I see a Lonerganian or Rahnerian analysis of conscience definitely pitching in on the side of women's rights. The data that support women's equality with men certainly weigh more heavily or ring more authentic than the data that would make woman the weaker vessel or primary agent of original sin (human twistedness). The tradition that has reserved Catholic priesthood to men certainly shows many purely human, culturally conditioned twists and turns, as it has come down to us from very patriarchal beginnings. On the other hand, the desire of significant numbers of Catholic women to serve in the formal ministry, though certainly it shows admixtures of all too human impurities, brings forth nothing that greatly distinguishes it from the similar desire of Catholic men. In my opinion, therefore, Catholic Christianity is inauthentic or underdeveloped in its opposition to institutionalizing, in terms of its structural power, the equality of women with men. I think that the primary site of the Holy Spirit, individual conscience—spiritual light and love—is much more congenial to feminists' arguments in this matter than to the arguments of resistant church traditionalists. By today's standards of light and love, Catholic Christianity comes out sexist: biased against women to a sinful degree. Its own canons of justice, honesty, love, and historicity tell against it.

The same criterion, fidelity to conscience, makes me view the stand of pro-abortionists darkly. Just as I must admit that some church leaders no doubt believe they are serving honesty and love by opposing women's ordination, so I must admit that some feminists no doubt believe they are serving justice and love by promoting the liberty of women to abort their children. Neither group, in my opinion, can stand up to a clear-eyed analysis of the dynamics of conscience. If the church officials stand revealed as people more concerned about legal traditions than people trying to secure the Christian community the best possible ministry (let alone as people especially solicitous of women's rights and anxious to make amends for the role the institutional church has played in women's historic oppression), the feminists strongly arguing for women's liberty to abort stand revealed as people who have preferred the (possibly or at most probably) improved welfare of mothers to the existence, the bare life, of the prenatal child. That preference does not compute, according to any standards of light and love that I find the dynamic structure of the human spirit producing. To maintain such a preference, one must in effect try to block out the existence of the prenatal child as a somewhat separate entity, the finality of the process of gestation (a being as human as its parents), and the character of the aborting intervention: killing. I don't think one can block out such basic facts and moral issues in good conscience. I think one must foster a culpable abstraction, aversion of attention, muddying of language, and thumping of ideological drums.

By way of counter-argument, I can hear staunch secular feminists saying that in very good conscience they don't believe in God and the sort of objective moral order that stems from a revealed, historical deity. Further, I can hear them charging that people like me avert their eyes from the concrete circumstances of many pregnant women, who are poor, already overburdened, and possessed of few resources for assuring the child they are carrying a good future. No doubt there is merit in this charge, and were we to converse as ideally we would, I would as much have to come to grips with the actual realities of women unwillingly pregnant as pro-abortion feminists would have to come to grips with the actual realities of killing prenatal human life. Then my programs for prevention, adoption, and education would no doubt acquire a sharper edge of realism. On the other hand, my charges that prenatal children deserve protection against being killed also should be sharper and more compelling.

So it would go, a debate or mutual exegesis that stayed close to the dynamics of conscience. On the question of God and a consequently objective moral order, we would again have to go beyond words or unchallenged self-interpretations, looking more at what people actually do and actually suppose than at what they say they do or what they say they believe. For example, on the whole most people act as though human life were a nearly ultimate value or good—something that morally can be sacrificed only in extreme case for overwhelmingly good reasons. Warmakers try to summon such reasons, but seldom have the makers of the wars that have bloodied history convinced responsible ethicians that they had satisfied the criteria of theories such as that of the just war. Murderers have virtually no justification for their taking of another human being's life except self-defense: the person was guilty of attempting to kill or seriously injure them. But what is the justification brought forth in the typical case of abortion? That the birth of this child will work a great hardship on the mother or the family into which it would come. Giving the child up for adoption is an obvious response to this claim. In broader perspective, making people responsible for their sexuality is the radical solution. As long as the prenatal child is human and innocent, however, virtually nothing justifies its destruction. The dynamics of conscience, it turns out, are more objective and demanding than what most people like. If studied with any thoroughness and integrity, they show that morality is not doing what we feel is right or think would be better, it is doing what we know conforms with intelligence, reasonableness, and love. The theist claims that if one accepts this reading of conscience the mystery at the foundations and borders of human existence becomes best interpreted as a transcendent divinity. The secularist may not be able to follow the process so far, but even acknowledging the mystery, and perhaps also the holiness or ultimacy, of conscience will take the secularist far away from casual abortion or the killing of prenatal children on demand.[5]

How does this exposition of authenticity relate to the expositions of Lady Wisdom and Catholic radicalism which it follows? I see the three as different expressions or versions of the Catholic Christian way of reading the signs posted at the intersection of human awareness and divine mystery. Certainly I view these signs through the lens of the Bible and the Christ. Certainly I have a bias in favor of placing temporal matters in the framework of a divine Kingdom or heaven. But the data of conscience themselves, I submit, shout that only the mysterious rootage of our reflective awareness places what we do and are in proper perspective. The data of the Incarnation, to which we now turn, elevate the perspective to a God's eye view of love.

· HOLY ABANDONMENT ·

The question put to all of us by death is whether we have used our experience of the mystery undergirding life to nourish a love and trust strong enough to warrant our letting go, our giving over, our abandoning ourselves to a silent Father or Mother. The Christian specification of this attitude is nothing less graphic than Jesus at his last breath on the cross: "Then Jesus, crying with a loud voice, said, 'Father, into thy hands I commit my spirit'! And having said this he breathed his last" (Luke 23:46). Catholic Christianity, along with the other Christian traditions, interprets this final surrender in the light of both Jesus' resurrection and what later theology defined about his inmost identity as the incarnate Word of God. Feminists, I submit, would do well to take it as an invitation to anticipate and inspect the end of human life that they may find many reasons for hope.

We come into the world apart from our own volition, and we leave the world at a time and in a way not of our own choosing (unless we commit suicide). A great many of the things that happen to us as we pass along the arc between these two terminal points are not things we choose. Human life, in other words, is a passion as much if not more than an action. The existentialists who pictured human life as a project of self-making told perhaps half the story well, but they neglected the half of at least equal significance. Indeed, if one weighs the way we enter and leave the world more heavily than what we make of ourselves while here, our passion, like that of Jesus, has the more important affect on our meaning.

It is a commonplace, in fact, to find New Testament scholars speaking of the gospels as passion narratives with a brief setting of the stage. The end of Jesus, his passover from death as a criminal to first born from the dead and Lord of all, determined what his disciples made of his birth and public ministry. Along with their experience of the Spirit and the risen Christ in their local Christian communities, the early followers of the Christian way oriented themselves by Jesus' end. Paul, in fact, virtually ignored Jesus' earthly life, shaping his entire theology in terms of Jesus' death and resurrection.

This suggests that a Catholic feminist spirituality, perhaps running considerably against the grain of contemporary thought, must make thorough provision for the end of a human life's project. Whether the consideration is something focused like ordination on the common good of the Christian community, or something as wrenching as ending the life of an unborn child, the abandonment that a faithful, hopeful, loving contemplation of the *eschata*, or last things, recommends will always be relevant. Jesus did not hand himself over to the Father on the cross in an act eccentric to the rest of his life. As the disciples and evangelists remembered it, his death simply consummated the way he had lived and preached and taught and healed. For the synoptics, his constant preoccupation was the Kingdom of God, the reign of the Father that he thought was at hand. For the author of John, his constant preoccupation was his relation to his heavenly Father. The end of Jesus merely dramatized or brought home to the disciples beyond any doubt (and we should not underestimate the dullness of the disciples, since the New Testament does not) the other-worldly reference that made Jesus who he was.

The disciples of Christ, today, face a world and a human destiny that differs from those of Jesus in no detail of truly ultimate significance. Camus could say a generation ago, "People die and they are not happy." Jesus wanted to change that for his contemporaries, and he has changed that for all who have allowed him to, letting his Father love them and do what he would. Feminists who feel so inclined should rewrite this sort of biblically based paragraph so that

God emerges as a nursing mother whom they could not imagine abandoning her child. People who feel strung out by a church that depreciates femininity or by a society that terminates prenatal life casually should be sure to take their sorely tried spirits to the ultimate mystery and try to hand them over in trust. One who is not sanguine that her church will soon come up to the mark of feminist love of equality, as one who is not sanguine that her society will soon reverse its tolerance of abortion, should try to hand these messes fully over to God. The mother who has aborted a child and suffered ever since, like the woman who has wanted to serve as a Catholic priest for painfully long, has a clear and present burden to hand over. The mystery challenges us to challenge it. When life has finally made a mockery of our pretensions to self-sufficiency, blessing our drives to be responsible and autonomous but showing us that in fact we don't have the last word, we shall have to take our stance with regard to the mystery and say our yea or nay. Blessed and wise are we if we start to face up to this demand and process before we find ourselves tented in intensive care. Blessed and wise are we if we let the silence of the dark pre-dawn or the silence of the late night hours, when only the sighs of the wind and the creaks of the house intrude, settle our spirits and position our meditations.

Catholic feminism should use the freedom of ultimate perspectives and a love that abandons worldly cares to reach the peace of a Saint Teresa: Let nothing disturb you. It should use the vivid icon of Jesus, bloodied yet still beautiful, to help it love the flesh God has given to women and through women, love the life that people can make in homes that are faithful, churches that are caring, works and services that open themselves to divine creativity. When closeness to God reveals a social system woefully careless of life and those whose hold on life is most vulnerable, Catholic feminism should be in advance of its male leadership in speaking out, since the majority of those neglected and threatened are sure to be women and children. Whether the matter be aid to dependent children, treatment of people in nursing homes, policies of war and deterrence, or theological treatments of sexuality, Catholic feminists can be sure that their twofold allegiance to a sacramental Christianity and the full humanity of women will make their voice prophetic.

What is prophetic is not necessarily welcome, of course. Indeed, frequently it is positively unwelcome, even when it is surely the small, still voice of Lady Wisdom, not trying to compete with the hard-driving whirlwinds. But the job of the prophet or prophetess is not to win welcome but to announce the Word of repentance and grace. The job of the prophet is to believe publicly, out in front of the many, and detail the specific changes this belief implies.

So, heard or unheard, honored or dishonored, the prophet should go her way, trying hard to learn from her experience and amend her defects of judgment and character, but trying even harder not to break faith with the Word by which she lives. What is the Word by which we live? That varies from person to person, of course, but all people will find the question a relevant prod to a fruitful examination of conscience. As I see Catholic Christianity (no different in this from any other Christian tradition mindful of the Bible), only Jesus has the words of eternal life and so deserves designation as the Word that came down from the Father (the question of salvation through other world religions is only a distraction at this point, but of course I think that saving grace is available to all people). The task and opportunity I see confronting Catholic Christian feminists now is appropriating the femininity of the Word much more fully. For two thousand years the official appropriations have been masculine, to an unbalanced degree. Now history has evolved to a juncture at which women's interest in sharing the imaging of God and humanity's need of cultural shifts away from death toward life virtually coincide. The two ways, of death and life, have seldom been counterpoised more clearly. Therefore, let us choose life, abandoning all our lesser gods to the consuming fire of the divine love: the Spirit of God that was moving over the waters and brooding new life.

NOTES

Chapter 1: Introduction

1. See Eric Voegelin, *Anamnesis* (Notre Dame, IN: University of Notre Dame Press, 1978), especially pp. 89–115.

2. See Heinrich Fries and Karl Rahner, *Unity of the Churches: An Actual Possibility* (New York: Paulist/Philadelphia: Fortress, 1985), pp. 25–42.

3. See Karl Rahner, *Foundations of Christian Faith* (New York: Seabury, 1978), pp. 448–60.

4. See Rosemary Haughton, *The Passionate God* (New York: Paulist, 1981).

Introduction to Part I

1. See, for instance, Bernard Cooke, *Ministry to Word and Sacraments: History and Theology* (Philadelphia: Fortress, 1976).

2. See Elisabeth Schüssler-Fiorenza, *In Memory of Her* (New York: Crossroad, 1983).

Chapter 2: Christian Ministry

1. Edward Schillebeeckx, *The Church with a Human Face* (New York: Crossroad, 1985), p. 32.

2. See Sergio Torres and John Eagleson, eds., *The Challenge of Basic Christian Communities*, (Maryknoll, NY: Orbis, 1981).

3. Ernesto Cardenal, *The Gospel in Solentiname*, vol. 3 (Maryknoll, NY: Orbis, 1979), pp. 70–71.

4. See Alice Walker, *The Color Purple* (New York: Washington Square, 1982).

Chapter 3: Women's Work

1. See Carol Gilligan, *In a Different Voice* (Cambridge, MA: Harvard University Press, 1982).

2. See Thomas Groome, *Christian Religious Education* (San Francisco: Harper & Row, 1980).

3. See Leonardo Boff, *Church: Charism and Power* (New York: Crossroad, 1985).

4. See Raymond E. Brown, *The Community of the Beloved Disciple* (New York: Paulist, 1979).

Chapter 4: Women's Leadership

1. Jonathan Schell, *The Fate of the Earth* (New York: Knopf, 1982).

2. Jonathan Schell, *The Abolition* (New York: Knopf, 1984).

3. Alan Paton, *Ah, But Your Land Is Beautiful* (New York: Charles Scribner's Sons, 1982).

4. Doris Lessing, *Shikasta* (New York: Knopf, 1979).

Women's Priesthood

1. Lawrence S. Cunningham, *The Meaning of Saints* (San Francisco: Harper & Row, 1980); *The Catholic Heritage* (New York: Crossroad, 1983).

2. See Karl Rahner, *Concern for the Church* (New York: Crossroad, 1981), pp. 35–47; Elisabeth Schüssler-Fiorenza, "The Apostleship of Women in Early Christianity," in *Women Priests: A Catholic Commentary on the Vatican Declaration*, ed. Leonard Swidler and Arlene Swidler (New York: Paulist, 1977), pp. 135–40.

3. Lora Gross, "The Embodied Church," in *Women Ministers*, ed. Judith L. Weidman (San Francisco: Harper & Row, 1981), pp. 136, 138. The reference to James Nelson is to his book, *Embodiment: An Approach to Sexuality and Christian Theology* (Minneapolis: Augsburg, 1978).

4. See Andrew Greeley, Mary Durkin, David Tracy, John Shea, and William McCready, *Parish, Priest and People: New Leadership for the Local Church* (Chicago: Thomas More, 1981).

5. Emily C. Hewitt and Suzanne R. Hiatt, *Women Priests: Yes or No?* (New York: Seabury, 1973), pp. 95–96.

6. Haye van der Meer, S.J., *Women Priests in the Catholic Church? A Theological-Historical Investigation* (Philadelphia: Temple University Press, 1973), p. 117.

7. See Rosemary Ruether, *Sexism and God-Talk* (Boston: Beacon, 1983).

8. See William M. Thompson, *The Jesus Debate* (New York: Paulist, 1985).

9. Paul K. Jewett, *The Ordination of Women* (Grand Rapids, MI: Eerdmans, 1980), pp. 22–23.

10. Rosalie Muschal-Reinhardt, "The Assembly Speaks," in *Women and Catholic Priesthood: An Expanded Vision*, ed. Anne Marie Gardiner, S.S.N.D. (New York: Paulist, 1976), p. 187.

Chapter 6: Christian Theory

1. John T. Noonan, Jr., *A Private Choice* (New York: Free Press, 1979). For representative feminist objections to Noonan's analyses, see Beverly Wildung Harrison, *Our Right to Choose* (Boston: Beacon, 1983).

2. See David Hollenbach, *Claims in Conflict* (New York: Paulist, 1979), on the function of the dignity of the human person in recent Catholic Christian social teaching.

3. For a rundown of recent scholarly opinion on both the political and the theoretical dimensions of abortion, see Lisa Sowle Cahill, "Notes on Moral Theology: Abortion," *Theological Studies*, 46/1 (March 1985), pp. 64–74.

Chapter 7: Feminist Theory

1. Hunter College Women's Studies Collective, *Women's Realities, Women's Choices* (New York: Oxford University Press, 1983), p. 20.

2. See, for example, Mary Gordon, *Men and Angels* (New York: Random House, 1985).

3. See Mary Daly, *Gyn/Ecology* (Boston: Beacon, 1978).

4. Vern L. Bullough, *The Subordinate Sex* (Baltimore: Penguin, 1974).

5. Geoffrey Parrinder, *Sex in the World's Religions* (New York: Oxford University Press, 1980).

6. Denise Lardner Carmody, *Women and World Religions* (Nashville: Abingdon, 1979).

7. Rita Gross and Nancy Falk, *Unspoken Worlds* (San Francisco: Harper & Row, 1980).

8. Not fully serious, but insightful nonetheless, is John Updike's *The Witches of Eastwick* (New York: Knopf, 1984).

9. See Leonardo Boff, *Church: Charism and Power* (New York: Crossroad, 1985), p. 142.

10. Carol Gilligan, *In a Different Voice* (Cambridge, MA: Harvard University Press, 1982). For other cases and psychological profiles of

women contemplating abortion, see James Burtchaell, ed., *Abortion Parley* (Kansas City: Andrew and McMeel, 1980).

11. John T. Noonan, Jr., *A Private Choice* (New York: Free Press, 1979), pp. 87–88.

Chapter 8: Prudential Theology

1. See, for example, Sharon Bishop and Marjorie Weinzweig, eds., *Philosophy and Women* (Belmont, CA: Wadsworth, 1979).

2. See, for example, Charlene Spretnak, ed., *The Politics of Women's Spirituality* (Garden City, NY: Doubleday, 1982).

3. J. Grundel, "Birth Control, I," in *The Concise Dictionary of Christian Ethics*, ed., Bernard Stoeckle (New York: Seabury, 1979), pp. 26, 27.

4. See Mary G. Durkin, *Feast of Love: Pope John Paul II on Human Intimacy* (Chicago: Loyola University Press, 1983).

5. Good resources for fleshing out a balanced Catholic Christian position may be found in Sydney Callahan and Danial Callahan, eds., *Abortion: Understanding Differences* (New York: Plenum, 1984). This is a publication of the Hastings Center, whose magazine and members' other publications offer many helps on moral questions, especially those dealing with bio-ethics.

Chapter 9: Politics

1. See John T. Noonan, Jr., *A Private Choice* (New York: Free Press, 1979), pp. 20–32.

2. See Ronald Reagan, *Abortion and the Conscience of the Nation* (New York: Thomas Nelson, 1984).

3. Sandra M. Schneiders, "New Testament Reflections on Peace and Nuclear Arms," in *Catholics and Nuclear War*, ed., Philip J. Murnion (New York: Crossroad, 1983), p. 104.

Chapter 10: Conclusion

1. Eric Voegelin, *Order and History*, 4 vols., with a fifth posthumous volume due (Baton Rouge: Louisiana State University Press, 1956, 1957, 1957, 1974).

2. Mary Gordon, *Men and Angels* (New York: Random House, 1985), p. 16.

3. Rosemary Haughton, *The Passionate God* (New York: Paulist, 1981).

4. See Paul Brodeur, "Annals of Law (Asbestos)," *The New Yorker*, June 10, 17, 24, and July 1, 1985.

5. I would appreciate the opportunity to apply my criteria of authenticity at leisure and length to a work of feminist theory such as Rosalind Pollach Petchesky, *Abortion and Woman's Choice: The State, Sexuality, and Reproductive Freedom* (New York: Longman's, 1984). I doubt that the work would hold up, for it seems (on something less than perusal) blissfully unaware of such a fundamental and ultimate matter as the divine mystery that makes us human.